The Naked Fish

Ian Hansen grew up in Adelaide and Melbourne during the 1930s and 40s. He became a teacher during the 1950s, working both in Australia and England with his wife, Dorothy. Ian Hansen has three children and seven grandchildren and now lives in Melbourne.

For my children and grandchildren
that they may understand

the naked fish

an autobiography of belief

Ian Hansen

Wakefield
Press

Wakefield Press
17 Rundle Street
Kent Town
South Australia 5071

First published 2002

Printed and bound by Hyde Park Press, Adelaide

National Library of Australia
Cataloguing-in-publication entry

Hansen, I.V. (Ian Victor), 1929– .
The naked fish: an autobiography of belief.

ISBN 1 86254 593 6.

1. Hansen, I.V. (Ian Victor), 1929– . 2. Educators – Australia – Biography. I. Title.

370.92

Wakefield Press thanks Fox Creek Wines and Arts South Australia for their support.

Contents

The ultimate reader of one's autobiography is God, from whom it is idle to try to hide the truth.
J.M. Coetzee

Acknowledgements

Thanks are due to Fay Zwicky and the University of Queensland Press for permission to quote from one of her poems. I have to thank those people who, having read this story in manuscript, encouraged me to persevere, among them particularly Ada Cheung, Tim Costello, Norman Curry, Melville Edwards, Margaret and Edgar French, Ligia and Anya Roskam, Joyce Leigh and my two sons Peter and David. Very special thanks, however, must go to Barry Hill and Allan Patience, who not only kept me at the task but also made suggestions that were always helpful and insightful. And special thanks to Dorothy, who has contributed more than I can say, and not only to the book.

1. The First Problem

The Seacliff train pulled out of Brighton station and gathered speed as it approached the level crossing with its wig-wag warning signal ringing out. Then the train's whistle blew desperately because, standing alone at the crossing, was a boy aged about three and a half.

The little boy was I, was me, and I was engulfed by the noise and enthralled by the train's power.

I was waiting for the monster-noise to thunder up to me. And I was ready; I had a long stick in my hand, split off a paling fence. As the engine, wheels clattering, reached the crossing, its whistle shrieked again. The piston-chamber spat out steam, the rails bucked and the racket was deafeningly glorious as I held out my stick and felt it snapped and jerked by the spokes of the giant and dangerous wheels.

There were only three carriages and the last was reaching the crossing when I felt a terrible grip on my left arm, just above the elbow, and was wrenched off my feet and spun around. My stick was gone and a broad hand slammed at the seat of my overalls. And again – and again. And at intervals all the way across the box-thorn strewn paddocks that led to the dead end of Rutland Avenue.

My father's towering anger lay across me like a shadow all the way home.

I have no memories earlier than this one. We're told that first memories are significant, but the significance of this one escapes me. Was I seeking freedom when I wandered off across the paddocks? Did I want noise in place of a silent household? Would my father always be my rescuer? Would the threat of punishment hang over all my attempts at independence? None of these, I think. I was a little boy, not without some spirit of adventure; I'd been on the train with my parents, I knew trains, I liked trains. I wanted a train for myself. Not a toy, a real train. And I knew where to get one.

I lived at 22 Rutland Avenue, the manse of the Brighton Baptist Church, where my father was the minister. He always called himself 'the minister', never 'the pastor'. Did he see himself as servant rather than a shepherd?

The Reverend Norman Hansen had been at the Brighton church in Adelaide for three years when I was born. I was told much later that this occurred at midnight on 4 August 1929, but doctor and midwife were not sure of the exact time and registered my birth as Monday 5 August. It was the month when the Alice Springs to Adelaide railway line was completed, when the *Graf Zeppelin* airship completed a round-the-world voyage, and, of course, the whole of Australia was struggling through the Great Depression.

My arrival caused a fuss among my father's congregation. They would have known, via the holy gossip prevalent in churches, that my mother had already lost two babies: according to them, I was the special survivor.

As a baby I was cared for according to the Truby King method of child rearing. Dr Frederic Truby King was a New Zealand paediatrician who believed in regular feeding. That is, babies were to be fed, breast or bottle, at six o'clock, ten, two and so on, on the dot. Not at five to ten, or quarter past six, but at ten and six. A baby could scream with hunger for twenty minutes before feed-time, but mother had to be firm and not relent. This way, so King's argument ran, weight-gain could be monitored accurately. The Truby King regime became very popular among the educated middle classes in New Zealand, Australia and around the English-speaking world. I was a sickly infant and my parents were determined I would have every chance to grow into childhood. The method worked. I grew in strength, though whether in favour with God and Man is more than I can say.

But it was all at a cost. My later life, from childhood into adulthood, became riddled with obsessive behaviours. I was obsessively neat. I always put the same shoe on first and if I didn't it distressed me and I felt awkward. In my teens, pens and pencils at rest on my desk had to lie parallel with each other. I could not sleep unless my slippers were placed together in the same place every night. When I was in my thirties I met three academic colleagues, of my age, who had been Truby King babies as well, and we were all prone to obsessive behaviour. One of them, I remember, would untie his shoe laces throughout the day and check they were of equal length. None of us could bear to be late for an appointment.

But my well-meaning parents would have known nothing of these potential consequences, of course.

Unlike most other fathers, mine worked from home. He did his reading and sermon preparation at home, then cycled to his pastoral visits each afternoon for a couple of hours. The manse had a front door, rarely used, and a side door. This door, down the crunching gravel driveway, opened straight into my father's study, so people could visit him without having to pass through the house.

I soon became conscious that our home was oriented to the needs of Other People. The family wasn't just me and Mum and Dad. It meant the beginning of my sense of community. Just as well. Ours was a silent house. My mother, Lilian, was frail and prone to migraine headaches. She seemed often to be lying down in a darkened room. But an only child comes to enjoy its own company – there's no one to squabble with – and I got on in my own world. I had Teddy for company and, a measure of my forward-thinking mother, Dolly. We never had a dog in Brighton, but a canary, which seemed to whistle more than canaries do today.

In front of the manse was an expanse of buffalo lawn, which prickled my bare feet in a delicious way when I ran across it. Every now and then one of the church members, a very tall and elderly be-spectacled gentleman with a trim, white Edward VII beard, came to cut the lawn. He always wore a proper felt hat and a waistcoat with a golden watch chain and he cut our grass with a scythe. I remember sitting on the step of the front verandah (where I'd been told to sit), watching the rhythmical back and forth swing of his scythe.

Just as I reached school age I was allowed a rare excitement. The milkman, who delivered milk from a horse-drawn, two-wheeled cart, would run to the front door of each house, where the householder left an enamel billy-can, and ladle in whatever the order was for – a pint, two pints. When he leapt back onto the low-slung cart, the horse would amble on to the next house. My thrill was to get up early, dress, wait for the milkman at the top of the street, then ride with him the length of Rutland Avenue. When he ran into the houses, I was left in charge of the cart, holding the reins. It never occurred to me that the horse was trained to stand – I believed that I was in charge. Some mornings I imagined I was driving a Roman chariot into a grand colosseum as the horse nodded from house to house. It was the beginning of my imaginative adventures. Both my father and my mother read me all sorts of stories, and now I was starting to live in them.

My parents may have seen me as special, but my father was determined I should not be spoilt. I was to know my place and to have a proper estimate of myself. If I transgressed

I was to be punished. The instrument of my punishment was a piece of pine from the side of a wooden fruit box. It was three inches broad and made more noise than damage when applied to the seat of my pants. I remember the slap and sting of it when I'd broken the head of a dahlia in the back garden or told a lie. I'm not sure I resented it, it was just part of living, like my father's rough goodnight kiss or my mother's gentle care of a skinned knee.

Once, I remember, I rebelled. I don't recall the reason, but I anticipated the stick and locked myself in the toilet for two hours. At first there was a rattling of the door-handle and demands that I come out, but then silence, not even footsteps in the house. Had they gone away and left me? Finally my curiosity got the better of me. I ventured out into the kitchen, and found my mother there. 'Here I am,' I said brightly.

'So I see,' my mother replied and went on with what she was doing.

Somewhat disappointed, I went to my father's study and stood in the doorway. He looked around at me and then turned back to his writing pad. The silence was worse than the stick.

The focus of our week was Sunday: Sunday service and Sunday School. In morning church I sat with my mother two rows from the back on the left-hand side. During my father's sermon she would pass me paper and a pencil and I would spend the next twenty minutes (they were always twenty minutes long, the sermons, even to the end of my father's ministry) drawing and trying out words. I liked standing up for the singing of the hymns. The sound and the tunes washed all around me, like the train noise at the level crossing. I could just see over the back of the pew in front and I took in all the heartiness of the congregational singing.

The hymns fixed themselves in me, forever to be associated with that little red-brick Brighton church.

How pleased and blessed was I
To hear the people cry
'Come let us seek our God today'
Yes, with a cheerful zeal
We haste to Zion's hill
And there our vows and homage pay.

and

O worship the King
All-glorious above;
O gratefully sing
His power and his love;
Our Shield and Defender,
The Ancient of Days,
Pavilioned in splendour
And girded with praise.

There was grandeur and certainty in all that enthusiastic singing going on over my head. As I learned to read, it became the words that I loved – I scarcely knew what they meant but they *sounded* so well. And there was the last verse of our Hymn 577 (the 'How pleased and blest was I' one):

My tongue repeats her vows
Peace to this sacred house!
For there my friends and kindred dwell:
And since my glorious God
Makes thee His blest abode
My soul shall ever love thee well

'Friends and kindred' I liked, and 'dwell' and 'blest abode' were great words, I thought.

At the end of the service my father stood on the church steps farewelling the worshippers, and sometimes, when not playing with the other children on the tennis court next door, I stood with him. I recall, now with acute embarrassment, a well-meaning maiden lady patting me on the head and saying, half to my father, 'My, you are growing tall,' and me, with a flourish of pomposity, saying, 'Yes, and what's more important, I'm growing good.'

It was not long before I was being put in my place by my peers. Of the boys in our street I was the youngest. I got picked last for cricket, and always had the cap-gun that didn't work when we roamed around the box-thorn in the paddocks playing Cowboys and Indians. Late one afternoon, hearing the train whistle at the level-crossing, I said by way of conversation to Bob, 'What time does your dad's train get in?' and he replied, 'The train's not my dad's; it belongs to the South Australian Railways.' I was crushed.

Baptist unions of churches were a loose federation of congregations and the central body was chaired alternately by an elected ordained minister and by a layman.

In 1934, my first year at school, my father became President of the Baptist Union of South Australia. His reputation as a preacher was widespread and he was held in high esteem by his fellow ministers. He was later succeeded by a lay-president, the irascible but brilliant specialist physician, Dr F.S. Hone.

During Norman Hansen's presidency to Hone's vice-presidency they became close friends, their uncompromising style a common bond. Of all this I knew nothing. All I knew was that Dad was off to even more meetings at night than ever before, and when Mum went with him some tall (always tall) maiden lady from the congregation waited with me in the house for their return.

I'm not sure how my father held his place in the Baptist communities. He was only forty-one when he was President of the Union, a comparative youngster, I'd have thought, for those days. And his preaching? A few of his sermons from the early and mid-1930s were published in Baptist newspapers and they were utterly free of the pious phrases and the scriptural references associated with such a conservative and evangelical denomination. They had a kind of literary intelligence about them. He often drew quirky texts from the Old Testament like 'The smoking flax shall he not quench' (Isaiah 42:3) and 'When thou hearest a sound of a going in the tops of the mulberry trees, then bestir thyself' (2 Samuel 5:24).

Of my schooldays in Brighton I remember two things. On my walk up Brighton Road to school I passed a grain merchant's store out of which wafted the most wonderful fragrance of wheat, pollard, and bran, all beautiful, warm smells. I would go in through the huge open entrance and savour the sweet aroma, dipping my hands into the open bags and the wooden bins.

My other clear memory is of Miss Burge, Molly Burge, my teacher. She was, so it seemed to me, very tall and broad – my mother was tall, but slim and frail. Miss Burge had a built-up black boot on one foot and a loping limp as she moved about at the front of the classroom. Her face was the most beautiful face I had ever seen. When she smiled her eyes shone soft and gracious, and she drew a deep devotion from me. If it's possible for a small boy to fall in love, then I fell in love with Miss Burge.

Preachers' kids, PKs, had to get used to moving as their parson-fathers shifted from parish to parish, congregation to congregation. Methodist PKs probably suffered more than most as the circuit system meant moving every three years. Baptist PKs usually had five years in one place, but sometimes seven or ten years. Dad had been at the Brighton church for almost ten-and-a-half years when he received a 'call' (as the non-Conformist churches had it) to Northcote in Melbourne. He preached his farewell sermon to the Brighton congregation on Anzac Day, 1937. Many people didn't want him to go, and the last goodbyes were said at the Adelaide station platform two days later.

It was terribly exciting for me to be travelling by train all through the night to Melbourne and I just wished the *Overland* would leave. But scores of my parents' friends were milling and crowding around the entrance to our carriage. When at last the train so slowly and heavily slid out along the platforms the crowd waved and called out, and some people, I could see, were crying.

So it was a new manse, weatherboard, not brick, a new church, a new Sunday School, a new day-school. Especially new to me was the coldness of Melbourne winter mornings. If you stomped on the shallow frozen puddles in the bluestone gutters in the streets they shattered into crazy patterns. The boys I walked to school with taught me swear words. I would rehearse them, in my head, sometimes *sotto voce*, as I strolled like Shakespeare's schoolboy to the corner where I met my friends. I never tried the words out at home. Some instinct told me I was doing something wrong, even that the words were evil, and that gave me a shiver of excitement. I could be bad with the best of them. What was being a PK anyway? So I practised the bloodys and the damns and the shits and worse and felt that they added to my social stature.

We played a game at school with cigarette or chewing gum cards – the cigarette cards were better because they were stiffer. With a card between your index and second finger and up against the base of your thumb, you flicked it with a snap of the wrist towards the bottom of a fence or a wall. The card nearest in one round to the fence or wall was the winner and took all the others. Everyone had lucky cards, and if you lost you never gave your best card away but one from your store. Some boys had dozens of cards done up with an elastic band.

Collecting a series of cards of cricketers – or footballers or aeroplanes or ships – was a side-issue to the card-flicking game. Winning a round might mean you could get from your defeated opponents just the cards you needed to complete a series. Or you could simply swap – two cricketers for a footballer or whatever it was you needed for your set. There was a series of cards you got with chewing gum called Kings and Queens of England, and I was well on the way to completing my set. But there were always rare cards that only seldom came with your flat piece of grey gum. So you went on buying chewing gum in the hope of getting Queen Caroline or Stephen or whoever it was you needed.

Early one evening when I was eight, my mother asked me if I would go to the corner shop and buy half a pound of butter. 'But,' she said, 'I've only got a ten-shilling note. So there'll be lots of change.' Off into the fading light I went. I bought the half pound of butter and then watched amazed as the shopkeeper counted silver coin after silver coin into my hand. I was holding more money than I had ever seen, except in a church collection-plate. In a flash of inspiration, I realised that with this money I could get all the kings and queens of England I wanted. If I was lucky and the shop's stock allowed it, I could get a whole set in one shot. So I went to the box on the counter and, in trembling excitement, chose one card after another. I got everything I needed and then chose some duplicates that I could use in swaps. The shopkeeper took back my handful of change and returned me a two-shilling piece. Walking home I realised I had no use for the chewing gum, so I took the cards from each packet and threw the gum away. Back in our warm kitchen I gave Mum the butter and she asked for the change. I gave her the two shillings.

There should be more change than this, she said. No, that's all he gave me, that's all there was. She made a sequence of additions and subtractions and told me how much change I should have had. No, I said, my voice rising in pitch, that's all he gave me. Truly. Drawn to the kitchen by the intensity of our voices, Dad came in. What had I done with the money? he demanded. Nothing, I replied, but knew the game was up. Tears pricked at the back of my eyes. There was nothing for it and I confessed, told the whole sorry tale, with the full expectation that my bottom would sing and ring from the broad blows of my father's great hand.

Where are these cards? Dad asked quietly. Mum stood watching as I took them from my pocket and held them out to him. He pulled open the tray in the wood stove, which gave off intense heat from the white and golden embers. 'Put them in there, one at a time.'

'But, Dad,' I objected, 'it's the whole set, I've got the whole set. They're all here, Dad.'

'Put them in the fire.'

I began to drop them in, one at a time, face up, and watched sniffling as they grew brown at the edges, curled, then collapsed in ash. Edward III and Queen Anne shuddered in the inferno and disappeared with a puff. I kept turning to my father, but his face was granite.

I was left with Queen Mary and William IV, the rarest in the card sequence. 'Can I just keep these two?' I pleaded.

'No.'

As they went into the fire, Dad slammed the drawer of the stove shut. The incident was never spoken of again.

The first words I ever committed to memory – they had seeped into my consciousness from many repetitions in church – were the words of the Lord's Prayer in the King James version: 'Our Father, who art in heaven, hallowed be Thy name . . .' God *was*, as far as I was concerned. No one doubted the existence of God. We even knew where He was, up there in heaven, looking down on us, seeing all that we did. We even knew what He looked like: in the choir vestry or the deacons' room there was always a large lithograph of the Lord God in Majesty surrounded by rank upon rank of angels or suppliants or saints. God had a long white beard. God was great, God was unapproachable, God was the punisher.

Thinking of God as 'Our Father' was not something I found easy. In one way, it was acceptable: 'Vengeance is mine: I will repay, saith the Lord' made sense. Dad had wreaked vengeance on me for my wrong-doing. God chastises, disciplines, and castigates. Steal Mum's change and then tell lies about it and you deserve all you get.

Mum had been giving me sixpence for offering and I'd been spending it on chewing gum for cards. When the offering bag came around in Sunday School I'd plunge my hand deep in the bag so no one could see I wasn't putting anything in. I'd been getting away with this for months, and now it had caught up with me. God was punishing me and His agent was my father. My father was an instrument of the God of Judgement, who sat on a throne and passed sentence. But there was a contradiction. The cards we got at Sunday School had multi-coloured wreaths of flowers around words like 'God is Love'. The God of Judgement wasn't showing much love, I didn't think, and neither was my father. Dad was stern and seldom smiled. When he did smile there was something almost mocking about it, never soft and loving like Mum's smile. So my first religious experience was wrestling with this idea of God the Father.

Not that Dad wasn't kind. He played French cricket with me in the backyard, and made me the best rolled newspaper footballs you ever saw. We played kick to kick together. In front of the winter fire, me in my pyjamas, he read me stories from Arthur Mee's *Children's Encyclopedia*. But Mum was love.

God was something else again. God made things, made everything. As my piping voice had so often joined in singing:

All things bright and beautiful
All creatures great and small,
All things wise and wonderful
The Lord God made them all.

Each little flower that opens,
Each little bird that sings . . .

So it went on, mountains, rivers, sunsets, fruit, tall trees . . .

How great is God almighty
Who has made all things well.

God was Creator – where else did all the world come from? But if I saw waves breaking on a beach, seagulls wheeling, and the numberless grains of sand under my toes, I never thought of God. I knew that God was creatively immanent, was in all things. I accepted it, as I accepted the cycle of days and seasons. This may not have been the God of Love, but it was God all right. I had no problem with Him in Creation.

What I couldn't understand was this 'Our Father' business. I was not yet able to distinguish between the religious style of the Old and the New Testaments. The Father concept didn't mesh with my experience, either, as God as a God of Love or as God as my father. A loving God understands and forgives. But my father neither understood (or if he did, he didn't let on) nor forgave me. I was in my early twenties before I came to terms with the idea of God the Father. That was because I had come to understand my father a little and because I'd sorted out in my mind who Jesus was. It was the Old Testament become the New, really.

For now, however, the business of the chewing gum cards gave me my first religious insight. I had to think through the incident, or wanted to think it through. But the idea of paradox was intellectually beyond me, and a resolution, if there was to be one, would have to wait.

2. It's Not Fair!

A Saturday morning in 1938, with a watery November sun, and I sat on the back verandah with Jerry from down the street. He'd brought some of his comic books, and as he rummaged through mine, I glanced at his. We didn't speak. I felt tired. I hadn't felt tired when I got up but I did now. The comics weren't very interesting, so I lay down with my head on the back step, holding one of the books above me so as not to offend Jerry. It was heavy to hold. Just then my father came through.

'What are you doing there?'

'I feel tired,' I said.

'Well, if you're feeling tired, you'd better go to bed.'

'I think I will,' I replied, and with great effort rolled onto my knees and pulled myself up by the porch pillar. 'Bye, Jerry.'

The doctor came after lunch and several times asked me to squeeze his fingers with my right hand. 'Tighter! Tighter!' I squeezed until my head throbbed. He mumbled in the doorway to my mother and father and I thought I heard the word 'ambulance'.

Within the hour I was in a four-bed ward at the Fairfield Infectious Diseases Hospital. Towering above me like a huge black barrel was an iron lung. I was enveloped by something that was pumping at me with a regular rhythm.

Four days followed when I saw neither Mum nor Dad, when every time the nurse fed me with a spoon the mushy pap came out through my nose. Once, I remember, it was chopped spinach, and I'd never liked spinach.

I had contracted infantile paralysis, later to be called polio.

I was one victim in an epidemic that was sweeping Victoria, snatching children in an utterly random way. As it was simplistically explained to Mum and Dad, the virus had attacked my right hand, travelled up the arm, down the leg, then the left leg and the left arm and finally, almost spent, had lodged in my throat. No longer life-threatening, my condition was such that I could be sent home after a week, freeing my iron lung for someone who really needed it.

The polio epidemic had broken out in June 1937, spreading fear and even panic around Melbourne and across Victoria. Country towns were completely isolated when a case occurred and travellers on the roads told to turn back. Some schools, including mine, were closed for months at a time and sporting and social events were cancelled. Polio was a notifiable infectious disease; by the time I contracted it there were about 3000 children, most between the ages of two and ten, registered as victims. Police travelled from Sydney to patrol all crossings from Victoria into New South Wales in an attempt to confine the disease.

Dad had immediately contacted F.S. Hone, his Baptist friend in Adelaide, to ask for advice, and was alarmed when Hone made the trip to Melbourne to see me for himself. My father always wanted the best and Hone told him the best was Dr Jean Macnamara, a formidable physician in Spring Street. Her uncompromising initial advice was total immobility, to allow tissue to recover. So I was placed in an aluminium splint, and bandaged at feet and ankles, upper arms and forearms, with leather straps at the knees and around the waist; two firm padded leather pieces prevented me from turning my head. Twice a day my father unstrapped me and held me in a salt bath while my limbs floated uselessly.

Mine was an odd existence for the next twelve months or so. I began by calling for my mother whenever I had an itchy nose and then learned to put up with it. I remember the day when my head pieces were removed and I could look around the room at will. I remember the wonderful day when the bandage came off my left forearm: now I could scratch my nose myself. I remember the day when the bandage came off my left upper arm: now I could turn the pages of a book on a stand on my chest. Physical improvement was imperceptible. A physiotherapist came twice a week and then once a week, took me out of the splint and exercised my arms and legs, massaging them. She had long fingers and brightly painted fingernails. I'd never known anyone who had painted fingernails. She had shoulder-length blonde hair. I thought she was a film star.

A water-proof plaster cast was made for my right hand and forearm. It opened along the back and was able to be laced up. Once a week and then twice an ambulance took me to the Melbourne City Baths where I learned to swim ('The best exercise,' Dr Jean had said). I could swim before I walked again.

The impotence I felt when I stood for the first time has never left me. I quite forgot the blonde film star had her arm around me: I was fiercely angry, because my legs would not work, *would not* obey me. For a year I had lain spreadeagled in that splint, fantasising like a series of loop-films about playing half-forward for Footscray, about becoming a mountaineer, and here I was still being carried to the bathroom and the ambulance.

By now I had a pram, long and flat to take the splint, on a carriage of four wheels. I lay in the sun in the back garden, our Australian terrier Tiger across my legs, watching the fruit trees, reading and dreaming impossible dreams. Sometimes on Sunday afternoons teenage girls, never boys, would call after Sunday School and wheel me around the streets. The church people were very kind. They kept giving me postage stamps for my album, and soon I had what would become the basis of a substantial collection, particularly of Australian stamps.

Hours each day I was alone and immobile, with no one to talk to. I sank ever deeper into heroic fictions that became almost real for me. In day-dreams I rescued people from Mongolian bandits, from Red Indian war-braves, from rocky avalanches and snow-slides.

I also thought about God a lot. If God did everything, as I believed, why, then, did He do this to me? I thought all things were to be bright and beautiful and here I was, strapped in my splint and only able to dream about footy and cricket and chasey. I couldn't believe, I didn't want to believe, that God was punishing me for something. Surely not for spending Mum's change to get chewing gum cards? My mind would race around ideas like these, then suddenly I'd launch into another rescue fantasy and feel better.

I have a very early memory (was I four?) of opening the wardrobe in my parents' bedroom (moth balls, I remember) and gazing up at a military uniform hanging there. There was an officer's tunic, with a strip of medal ribbons above the left breast pocket, and a pair of riding breeches. On the shelf above was a Sam Browne belt, a pair of brown leather leggings, all the brass buckles gleaming, and a cap with bright gold leaves ringing the peak. Each Anzac Day I would wonder at my father as he returned from a dawn service. He was a part-time Army Chaplain: he dressed in uniform for special occasions and went to camp somewhere once a year.

In 1939 Dad was still a chaplain. My bed was in the front room of the manse, which under normal circumstances would have been our sitting-room; it offered more space than my bedroom. Dad came home after the Sunday evening service on 3 September and he and Mum listened to the late news on the wireless in the front room. I recall Menzies' voice clearly: 'It is my melancholy duty ...' he said, telling the Australian people that we were at war with Germany. My father sat stock-still, sucked at his pipe, and said nothing.

Within months Dad was promoted from Chaplain 2nd Class to Chaplain 1st Class and then to Chaplain-General (OPD): the OPDs were the Other Protestant Denominations, that is, Methodists, Presbyterians, Baptists, Churches of Christ, all those other than Roman Catholics and Anglicans. Now the Army needed more of his time. In April, May and June of 1940 he was in army camps full-time and a theological student took care of the Northcote church's affairs.

Mum was on her own, with the responsibility of caring for me. My mother was never robust. I wonder now whether the two still-births before me had damaged her health. She had to lie down for an hour or so each day; she was thin, her face drawn.

By now I could walk unaided, could get to Sunday School. I worked through my Correspondence School lessons with Mum's help (she was a trained primary teacher), but lacked the physical energy to go to 'real' school. I don't know how the domestic chores were divided in our house: Dad did the clothes washing, but that's all I remember. Obviously I couldn't be much help. Mum struggled on until Dad got back from camp and then, barely three weeks after his return, she was dead.

I remember that day. A Friday. The first I knew something was up was when my father came off the phone and told me I was to go to a church family for lunch. 'Your mother's not well.' Of course she wasn't well. I'd never known her really well. So why was I being sent off?

The couple whose house I was to visit lived near the

Northcote brickworks, which meant (for me) a long walk. Long enough to think a lot. The sky was a uniform, leaden grey. She's going to die, I thought, Mum's going to die. I didn't feel at all afraid as I walked on. The wind was sharp and gusty. If anything, I felt angry. Not sorrowful, sad or lonely, just angry. I didn't think about Dad and how he would feel when Mum died. I had a deep sense of angry resignation, if there is such an emotion. Resentment, perhaps. She'll die and then what? So what? I can even now see the corrugated iron fence I was passing when I felt so boldly resigned. It was a terrible set of thoughts for an eleven-year-old to have. I was so hard, hard of heart. I didn't know that my mother was only a few months off forty-six. By the time I reached High Street I knew she had died.

The next Sunday, two days later, was the strangest I had ever known. Dad and I didn't go to church; the young student took the services. I didn't go to Christian Endeavour or Sunday School, either. We just stayed home. Someone from the church brought a casserole for Dad to heat up and we kept away from each other. Dad was either in his study or standing vacant in the back garden; I was in my room, reading comics or browsing through the Arthur Mee's encyclopedia. Once or twice during our silent meals my father urged me to be brave, though why and what for was never explained. 'We'll be all right, son, somehow,' he said.

The funeral service was held during the week at the manse and the cemetery, but I never went. I suppose Dad wanted to deal with it on his own. The next Sunday he was back in the pulpit. At the end of that next Sunday morning service I stood with him in the porch while people awkwardly and wordlessly touched me on the head or shoulder. Some instinct told me Dad should be crying or feeling miserable, but he was just the same. His stoicism was remarkable.

He had been born in Port Melbourne into a strict Brethren family. The Brethren were an inward-looking, closed community, fundamentalist biblical literalists. Utterly convinced of their cause in the world, they were suspicious of any other Christian denomination. They had no clergy and conducted their affairs through laymen (women were of little account). Smoking and drinking were banned. Women wore no make-up and wound their long hair into a tight bun. There was no place for frivolity of any kind, in behaviour or dress. My father, his brothers and his sister must have endured this regime uncomplainingly as they grew up; it was the only life and world-view they knew. Their Port Melbourne Brethren Assembly or Meeting were in fact Hopkinites. That is, they were a Brethren sect of *peculiar* strictness who would have nothing to do even with other Brethren groups.

Around the Marshall Shoe Company's factory where my father worked and around the district, word went out that Norman Hansen was a more than useful medium-fast bowler. The Port Melbourne Baptist Cricket Club persuaded him to participate in a competition that was at that time of a fairly high order. After practice matches, Dad had three formal games with the club.

One Sunday evening each month all the team would attend a 'parade' at the Baptist Church's service. So it happened that on a certain Sunday afternoon Dad told his father, a Brethren elder, that he would not be attending the Meeting that night because he was required to be at the cricket team's parade with the Baptists. With that conviction in his voice that fundamentalists use, his father said to him that if he insisted on going to the church parade, he, Tom Hansen, would 'name' him before the Brethren the next Sunday. Not believing for a moment that his father would be so unfeeling, Dad went to the Baptist church that evening.

Next Sunday, at the morning Meeting, his father 'named' him; told the little community that his own son had deserted the Meeting for a Baptist service. He reminded the brethren and sisters of the importance before God of keeping the true faith and that that they should pray for Norman in his sin, pray him back into the Kingdom. Appalled, Norman walked out of the Meeting, never to return.

I can't imagine what this must have meant in the Hansen household. There must have been awful silences, strained conversations, flares of impatience and anger. For Dad, it was a kind of excommunication that he had to live with under that roof for week after week.

On turning twenty-one Dad offered himself as a lay missionary to the South Australian Baptist Union, was accepted, left home and began preaching and pastoral work in South Australia, serving little congregations in the Mallee settlements of Peake and Jabuk. He shared a two-room tin dwelling with his horse; Dad had the floorboards. The next year, 1914, he moved to the mid-north to Terowie.

I called the Brethren fundamentalist literalists and that perhaps needs an explanation. They (and not only they: all Protestant denominations have believers like them) hold rather grimly to a Bible verse from the Second Letter of Timothy: 'All scripture is given by inspiration of God, and is profitable for doctrine, for reproof, for correction, for instruction in righteousness'. They therefore put great store by verses like the one from Paul's letter to the Ephesians that says, 'Wives, submit yourselves unto your own husbands as unto the Lord'. And God worked for six literal days to create the world and all that is in it; no room here for Darwinism or scientific enquiry. The Bible becomes the source of all that one needs to know and, 'by inspiration of God', also provides political commentary, and guidance in times of uncertainty. During World War II the Brethren made much of the figure of the bear in Daniel's prophecy: the bear was Stalin's Russia.

I remember my father telling me about a minister from Sydney who had just taken up a pastorate in Adelaide. This earnest young man told his new congregation how wonderfully certain he was that God had led him there – after all, he had read at the breakfast table from Ezekiel: 'Moreover the word of the Lord came unto me, saying, Set thy face toward the south . . .' So why didn't he end up in Hobart? Dad said.

Of all the books of the Bible, the one that lends itself to extravagant interpretation is the Revelation of St John the Divine. It's been mined for centuries by commentators and preachers, and minerals torn from it have triggered farcical behaviours. There is the story, for example, of a Lutheran pastor in the Barossa Valley last century who, with his people, took literally the verses from Revelation 20 that say: 'And I saw an angel come down from heaven, and having the key of the bottomless pit and a great chain in his hand. And he laid hold on the dragon, that old Serpent, which is the Devil, and Satan, and bound him a thousand years'. The pastor had the local blacksmith fashion some large chains, then with his flock took them to the summit of the Kaiserstuhl, where they waited for Satan, intending to bind him in the chains and imprison him in the Barossa village of Langmeil.

And there is that mysterious verse in chapter 13: 'Here is wisdom. Let him that hath understanding count the number of the beast: for it is the number of a man; and his number is six hundred three score and six'. The beast has been interpreted by Protestants as the Pope, to which Roman Catholics have responded by finding in that 666 a reference to Martin Luther; 666 has been taken by other extremists as a signifier for Napoleon or Hitler or Stalin or even Bill Clinton.

The Brethren would have been comfortable with all of this, differing only in specific interpretations. Their faith was rooted in a literal view of the Bible and of the prophetic power (in the sense of looking into the future) of the Hoseas and the Daniels and the Ezekiels. With this my father had grown up.

Now he is living in Terowie, just off the main road, reading (I guess at this because of the inscription on the flyleaf, 'N.V. Hansen. Terowie,1914') a book by Frederic C. Spurr entitled *The Age-Long Struggle: Christ or Caesar*. It's a study of the Book of the Revelation. But it's not the kind of study that would suit the Brethren or many Australian Baptists – or Methodists or Presbyterians, for that matter. Spurr, pastor of the Collins Street Baptist Church, Melbourne, presents a tightly argued case that Revelation is a political tract dealing with the moral conflict between Caesarism and Christianity. Dad turns over to page fifty and reads:

> The whole of the writing crystallises around the figures 3, 4, 7 and 12 with their variants and extensions. A great part of the literary material is arranged on numerical lines. It does not require much insight that to understand a book thus constructed is an artistic book, and was never intended to be taken literally. 'History does not run in cycles of 7'. When events are deliberately grouped in threes, fours, sevens, and dozens, it is perfectly evident that we are in the realm, not of palpable facts, but of religious ideas . . .

Dad thinks long and hard. This is exciting, refreshing. He wants more. Because the South Australian Baptist Union doesn't have its own theological college, he enrols in 1915 in the Baptist College of Victoria, his tuition and board paid for by the South Australian Union of Churches. But by mid-year his mind is on other matters. The war in Europe is obviously not going to be over by Christmas. Because of religious scruples he doesn't want to be a combatant, and so in October 1915 he embarks for Egypt with the 4th Field Ambulance of the Australian Army Medical Corps.

Norman was in Egypt for nearly a year, in Cairo, Abbassia and Mustapha, his medical orderly work coming in waves. Wounded men from the eighth-month heroic debacle of Gallipoli filled military hospital beds to the end of 1915. Light horsemen suffered riding accidents and in August of 1916 were fighting in Sinai. In the middle of all this bandaging and dressing and patching came news from France, where other Diggers were grappling with the Hun. Stories filtered into the ambulance units in Egypt of the Battle of the Somme, of the appalling loss of Australian life at Fromelles, of the bitter struggle for the demolished village of Pozieres. Lance-Corporal Norm Hansen was becoming ever more angry and impatient. On 3 September he transferred to the famous 7th Battalion, an infantry outfit, and in three days was in the battlefield in France.

Eight weeks prior to Norman's arrival, his 7th Battalion had been part of the AIF's 5th Division flung into the ill-conceived attack on the French village of Fromelles. The 5th Division suffered 5533 casualties in a single night, equivalent to the entire Australian casualties of the Boer, Korean and Vietnam wars put together. In the fighting around Moquet Farm in late August and the first days of September the 7th Battalion had lost thirteen officers and 210 men killed or wounded, and it was this battered unit that my father joined.

Dad had joined the battalion after a summer of unseasonable heavy rain. The ground was so sodden that the walls of the trenches continually collapsed. Troops were up to their knees in mud. Rations came to them cold, for there was no way fires could be used in the front line. The grey and black skies went on raining. Three weeks after meeting his platoon, Lance-Corporal Hansen was, with four other platoons, ordered to enter the German lines north-east of what was called The Bluff. They engaged in hand-to-hand combat – bayonets and rifle-butts – with a German unit and returned with a handful of prisoners and no casualties of their own. It was Dad's first direct encounter with the enemy. He had four unbroken months of this sort of thing, right up until Boxing Day.

After seventeen days behind the lines, he returned to the Front in mid-January. Snow fell and lay thick for exactly a month in this appalling winter. There were hard frosts; icicles hung from the entrances to dugouts and on the barbed wire. Men suffered frost-bite to fingers and toes. When the snow thawed, they spent hours and days standing in cold mud and many of them contracted trench-foot, a kind of frost-bite. So it went on through 1917, an unending slog of attrition, gains of ground here, losses there.

Dad's longest stint in the field was eight months in 1918, from January to September. The British division that had been holding the Germans along two rivers in northern France since 9 April withdrew and was replaced by the Australian 5th Division. On the night of 12 April, the 7th Battalion was open to a massive German advance. It was part of the little-known but, as it turned out, significant Battle of the Lys. From Armentieres the River Lys ran westward and lay about ten kilometres from Fromelles. The German forces were moving from the north through Merville to the river. The 7th Battalion was ordered to take up and picket a front of some 6000 metres. Difficult but not impossible. Then the order was modified, and the officers and men suddenly found themselves strung out through the Nieppe

Forest along a front of nearly six and a half kilometres. A staff officer's comment in a despatch ran: 'the 7th Btn who are out in front somewhere with the enemy'. It must have been terrifying for this one battalion, thinly spread, waiting, while mortars thudded and field guns roared in the dark. Dad and his mates saw out the night and the days and weeks that followed. Lance-Corporal Hansen was promoted Corporal in late August, just as the great tide of the war turned. Suddenly, it was all over and the nightmare images of hands and legs protruding from mud and blind wounded groping along trenches faded in the euphoria of the Armistice in November.

Of all this I never heard a word from my father. What I've set down here I've researched for myself, from army records and the like. But a large, framed, sepia-toned photograph hung in his study in every manse that I can remember. It depicted a shattered landscape of broken tree trunks, with a line of duck-boards snaking across the mud. In the middle ground a tin-hatted soldier walked toward the photographer, rifle with fixed bayonet in his hand. Across his shoulder he was carrying the limp form of another soldier. I stared at the photograph countless times as I grew up, but I never asked about it. Somehow I sensed that it was private.

Why was it important to Dad? It was grim, terrible, with the silence of death about it, that awful frozen moment. These horrors Dad suppressed; he kept them buried deep, where they festered and churned. In this he was like thousands of returned soldiers of his generation. They called it shellshock in Dad's day, even cowardice when it all became too much and men lost their minds. Nobody thought to debrief them. On Anzac Day the veterans met and remembered cricket matches behind the lines, snooty Pommy officers or fierce French women serving wines and spirits, never the mud and the stench.

While the 7th Battalion was cleaning up in France and England, Dad was promoted to the officer rank of 2nd Lieutenant and then Lieutenant. He returned to the Baptist College of Victoria under the Soldiers' Repatriation Scheme. Arriving back from active service three weeks before the 1919 examinations began, he passed all three papers he sat with an average mark of seventy-one per cent and was commended by name by the interstate Church History examiner. It was a giant step from what he had known for the past four years.

Maybe his war experience had hardened him, steeled him in his relationships and his responses. He could not have been unfeeling, I realise now: people have always attested to his capacity for sensitive counselling. But here he was, a recent widower, carrying on without a murmur.

Lilian was gone. She'd been a teacher at the Port Melbourne Primary School and, importantly, at the Port Melbourne Baptist Sunday School, where she and Dad met. He had courted his Lil even from the trenches and, a year after he had been ordained to the ministry in the Hindmarsh church in Adelaide, he married 'Lilian Rose Kirkham Pinches, spinster' as the marriage certificate put it.

None of her grandchildren-to-be have given evidence of any genetic physical weakness, yet Lilian was never well. I guess, and I'm sure my father guessed, that motherhood damaged her irreparably. But she was gentle and kind, and during her brief bursts of good health was a bright, cheerful person to be with. Now she was gone. Did Dad have some slivers of guilt pricking his sorrow?

I hadn't gone back to school after my polio and still slept in my aluminium splint. Dad was involved in his Chaplain-General duties with the army and travelled to camps most weeks and some weekends. What would become of us?

3. Starting Afresh

We discovered part of the solution to our problem just round the corner from the church in Darebin Road, in the home of one of the congregation's widows, Min Ball (though I never dared call her Min). She lived with her daughter Dorothy and son John, who was eighteen months older than I. Dad would rent two rooms at the Balls', a study-cum-sitting-room and a bedroom. The rest of the solution was the boarding house of Carey Baptist Grammar School. I would go to Carey as a weekly boarder, and spend weekends with the Balls. That way, Dad could be free to undertake his chaplaincy duties as required, even over weekends, but would also be able to hold to his preaching and pastoral responsibilities at the church without having to undertake domestic chores.

For the next eighteen months or so it worked out well. I was at school during the week, Dad was mostly home at weekends, and we shared the bedroom.

At Carey for the third term in 1940 I had a space on the upstairs verandah of Urangeline, the noble Victorian mansion around which Carey had grown. It was my own space, because I had still (Dr Jean was insistent) to sleep in my splint, and the school accommodated my embarrassing needs. I was suddenly part of a great family and I loved it. I had mates of my own age, and a score of older brothers.

The headmaster was H.G. Steele, an uncompromising Baptist believer. Every night after the evening meal we had prayers in the boarders' lounge. When 'The Boss' took prayers, we always had a Bible reading followed by a homily based on the reading, usually urging us to be truthful, or understanding, or kind, or courageous for the faith (the school's motto was *Animo et Fide*, By Courage and Faith). Then we would kneel at our chairs pushed to the wall, while the Boss would kneel at the covered billiard table and pray extempore, Baptist fashion, for whatever took his spiritual fancy: Old Boys in the services, missionaries in India, the poor people of Melbourne, the need in our hearts, all of us, of the ever-forgiving Jesus. Then we repeated together the Lord's Prayer and the Boss pronounced

The grace of our Lord Jesus Christ
the love of God
and the fellowship of the Holy Spirit
be with us all, tonight
and for ever more.

We slid back onto our chairs and waited. Sometimes we had a notice or a reminder. Sometimes he just looked around and strode out of the room while we scrambled respectfully to our feet.

The Boss and his wife worshipped at the Kew Baptist Church, which held a prayer meeting each Wednesday evening. (Prayer meetings in all churches were always well attended during World War II.) So that the Steeles could go to their prayer meeting, Les Trewin, the boarding house master at Carey, took prayers. Prayers with Les were always the same. He'd pull out a familiar Bible reading from somewhere – the calling of Samuel, Jesus stilling the storm, or a short psalm. He'd offer no commentary, just announce 'Let us pray'. We'd fall to our knees and it was the general confession from the Book of Common Prayer:

Almighty and most merciful Father, We have erred and strayed from thy ways like lost sheep. We have followed too much the devices and desires of our own hearts, We have offended against thy holy laws, We have left undone those things which we ought to have done, And we have done those things which we ought not to have done . . .

Even though it was Les reciting it rather woodenly, I liked it. There was a certainty in the language. I knew I did things I shouldn't do and didn't do things I should. I wanted hereafter to live a godly, righteous and sober life, to the glory of God's holy name. And I wanted to live it in words like these. The prayers of intercession that the Boss prayed were all very well, but they were a simple conversation, as it were. I liked the rhythms and cadences of Les's repeated prayer. It should have been the other way round, I suppose: from a non-Conformist tradition I should have preferred the praying from the heart. Was it the strangeness of the Anglican formality that appealed? I don't know. I got over it: by my late teens it held no appeal at all. For the time, however, this motherless only-child loved the certain-sounding strength.

I felt wonderfully free at boarding school. Nobody fussed over me (no 'poor Ian') and each day was full of life and movement.

The polio meant I was no good at sport. I couldn't catch a ball in my right hand. I couldn't hold an overhead mark in football and I simply made up the numbers in scratch team games. Since excelling at sport in a sports-mad society was the way to popular success, I had to find some other way to distinction or notoriety. I found it in showing off and being smart. I must have been a trial to my weaker teachers. It was probably why I failed Scripture at the end of my first term at the school. We were taught by the Boss and I remember his remark as in the classroom he read out my exam results: 'And you a Baptist minister's son!'

I was caned once, for being part of a group of older boarders who caught a possum in a rabbit trap one of the country boys had brought back from holidays. The hapless possum was swinging down from the guttering by a back leg and I was detailed to despatch it with a hammer. The Boss caned me, but not before he delivered the Baptist minister's son jibe again.

I had one full school year at Carey. The Boss's jibe must have had some effect, for I was awarded two book prizes at Speech Night for committed work. My father smiled a crooked smile and said nothing.

If Carey spelt freedom, weekends with the Balls spelt fun. John and I went to the footy in the winter on Saturday afternoons. We had season tickets for the Northcote Football Club (though Football Association followers always supported a Victorian Football League team: mine was Footscray). We played French cricket in the back yard whenever we felt like it, winter or summer, and watched the two-up games that men played on waste ground over the lane at our back fence. One day there was a police raid, and we giggled together as men scampered over fences, around corners, and toward the back door of the Croxton Hotel. Most were confronted by men in blue, who frog-marched them down the lane and out into Darebin Road.

The church was the core of my social life. This was not because I happened to be the minister's son, but because it was the centre of the Balls' family life. Sundays had a lot going for them. The day began with Christian Endeavour. This was a movement begun in the United States with the aim of encouraging leadership in church children and teenagers. A leader ran a program that gave everyone the opportunity to take a public part. Someone did the Bible reading, someone gave out the notices, someone took up the offering, someone announced the hymns or the choruses. There was always a segment called 'sentence prayers' in which every child and teenager was expected to add a sentence to a chain of prayer. Keen Endeavourers would sometimes write out their piece beforehand. Most contributions, of course, were minimalist in nature: 'God bless the men in the Navy', or 'Hymn 9'. The words of choruses were imprinted indelibly on our minds, precepts and promises like 'Jesus wants me for a sunbeam . . . I'll be a sunbeam for him' and 'Look them out, get them gone, all the little rabbits in the fields of corn: Envy, jealousy, malice and pride, they must never in my heart abide'.

After forty-five minutes of Christian Endeavour there was a quarter of an hour for playing chasey around the tennis court or through the long grass at the back of the church hall. At eleven on the dot the morning church service began. Endeavourers sat with their parents (I sat with the Balls) and a third of the way through 'the children' were called to the front for the 'children's talk'. This was usually a five-minute homily supposedly pitched at a child's level, often an 'object lesson', when some 'object' like a rolling pin or a tram ticket served to focus minds upon great truths of the faith. My father wasn't very good at children's talks: he tried and was too earnest about them, generally finding them in preacher's help publications where the ideas were pretty sentimental anyway.

Still, it was a break, and during the singing of the 'children's hymn', usually something like

God who hath made the daisies
And every lovely thing
He will accept our praises
And hearken while we sing.

or

I love to hear the story
Which angel voices tell
How once the King of Glory
Came down on earth to dwell.

we returned to our seats. Rather than listen to the sermon, we read, something, anything. At the end of the service, with my father in the porch shaking hands, we resumed chasey around the buildings.

Sunday School was at three and ran for an hour. There were prizes for attendance. Lots of the kids' parents never came near the church: their offspring were packed off to Sunday School in the vague belief that it would be good for them. At least from what I remember, it couldn't have done them any harm. There was a syllabus to be followed by each class, so it was not a haphazard affair. Memory tells me that the teachers were mainly well-meaning 'maiden ladies'. The young male teachers were all off at the war.

By far the best part of Sunday School was the Sunday School Anniversary.

These were the 1940s. Sunday trading was almost unheard of, though you might find a milk bar open here or there. Few families had a motor car. On Sunday, the Lord's Day, the cinemas were shut and there were no sports fixtures of any kind. If it was entertainment you wanted, you made it yourself. You went for walks, or sat at home and read. Church was at least somewhere to go. Most people went to church; it was a kind of entertainment, a place of social intercourse. You would see knots of people chatting outside churches on Sunday mornings an hour after the service had ended.

But there was no entertainment quite like the Sunday School Anniversary. Our Sunday School scholars at Northcote numbered about seventy. For weeks before the anniversary date in September, Sunday School was given over to singing practice. We learned bouncy, youthful tunes from a printed collection of hymns and choruses under the fierce training of Mr Taylor, who would tick off anybody whose attention strayed from the beat of his baton. For weeks we were drilled without mercy, and then, on a Friday night, came the final practice. As if it wasn't exciting enough in itself to be going out at night, *the platform* had been erected. The platform was the *sine qua non* of Sunday School anniversaries. They all had one, the Methodists, the Churches of Christ. It consisted of tiered rows of timber (with the occasional splinter) bolted to metal scaffolding and ascending from the church floor up over the communion table and the baptistry, almost (it seemed) to the ceiling. It was rather like the stands erected for a coronation or grand prix. Smaller children sat on the lower rows and the older and oldest got to sit right up the top. At the final practice there was much foolery in and around the scaffolding until Mr Taylor brought us to order. Now, for the first time, we were to sing with 'the orchestra': a piano, two violins, a cello, a double bass, and once, I remember, a trumpet.

Come the Sunday morning, the season of praise began. This occasion was so special that it was the excuse and reason for a hair-cut and for new clothes. If you needed a new pair of trousers or new socks, you had to wait for the Sunday School Anniversary. The girls had new frocks or skirts or shoes or bows for their hair. The church ladies had spent hours on floral decorations, up and down the platform and around the orchestra. The building was a riot of colour, thanks to the flowers, neckties of the older boys and the girls' dresses, scarlet, blue, pink, gold. And we sang like angels.

In lieu of Dad's sermon, visiting preachers presented addresses tailored for the young. There must have been a circuit for Sunday School anniversary speakers. We would hear that one we had did his performance up the road at the Methodists' a couple of Sundays later. The preachers were generally laymen, spiritual entertainers who did extended 'object lessons'. One conjurer-speaker had us gasping at his disappearing billiard balls and miraculously appearing bright, silk handkerchiefs. A model-train buff, Mr Booker, brought his 00 gauge electric train and an extensive layout complete with tunnels, lakes, farms and villages. The train, with us on board, was bound for Heaven, stopping in at stations with names like TEMPTATION and DOUBT. It was a kind of *Pilgrim's Progress* on wheels. We loved it.

Our anniversary services packed them in. The pews were full a quarter of an hour before starting time and chairs would be rushed in down the two aisles until people had to stand in the porch to listen. This went on three times a Sunday for two Sundays, six performances, a veritable season of pious witness to our faith, or whatever it was we were told we believed in. We sang and sang about love and trust and forgiveness and hope. And the congregation become audience loved it.

Next on the agenda after the anniversary was the annual Sunday School Picnic. It was held on Melbourne Cup Day, a convenient public holiday for those like us who had no interest in the sinful horse race that encouraged gambling. Sunday School teachers and the ladies of the church were up just after dawn in the church hall making sandwiches by the hundreds. Trays of lamingtons and butterfly cakes appeared, tea urns were brought out and dusted and wiped clean, raspberry cordial was made up in big kerosene tins. By half-past eight a line of four furniture vans had drawn up in High Street in front of the church. We children were already milling about excitedly on the tennis-court, and by a quarter to nine we were being shepherded by class into the vans. Up into the cavernous space we scrambled, climbed or were lifted, then squeezed onto benches down each side. A tray at the van's rear was slammed shut, and we were off to some place we thought was away in the country – once, I remember, to Kangaroo Ground, beyond Warrandyte.

There was always a program for the day: fifty-yard sprints for children, fathers, even mothers, egg and spoon races, sack races, three-legged races. We'd play a cricket match. Ropes thrown over a tree branch became swings for small children. Lunch was served from trestle tables, all those sandwiches and cakes which, after singing grace, we sat on the grass and dried gum leaves to eat. And then the cordial, bright pink or golden green, for which we queued in long lines.

By mid-afternoon our energy was flagging. Games of hidey and tiggy became desultory. Older boys and girls paired off and drifted to the margins of the picnic ground to hold hands or tentatively kiss in the shadows. Rallied together before boarding the furniture vans, we – all of us, the scholars, teachers, parents – sang:

Blest be the tie that binds
Our hearts in Christian Love;
The fellowship of kindred minds
Is like to that above.

On the drive home, encouraged by our teachers who sat with us in the vans, we sang our anniversary songs: with all the practising we'd had, we knew all the words of all the verses. So it was that, in the cliché we would use in a school essay account of the occasion, 'we returned home tired but happy'.

I was feeling happy most of the time now. Being at the Balls' was fun. The wireless was always on, playing Glenn Miller and Artie Shaw and Bob Crosby's Bobcats. We hummed 'A Nightingale Sang in Berkeley Square' and 'The White Cliffs of Dover'. I played 'In the Mood' and 'Boogie Woogie Bugle Boy' in my head over and over again. Every Friday night was fish and chips and we sat around the kitchen table laughing for ages. One night, after we'd finished the dishes, big, shapely Dorothy got on the table to tap-dance, with her skirt flaring out. It was the first time I'd seen a suspender belt and lace panties. And she was a church girl. Times at the Balls' were best when Dad wasn't there, when he was at Puckapunyal Army Camp or somewhere.

Mrs Ball and Dorothy went to church in the evenings, leaving John and me at home for the hour or so. We didn't go because the evening service was reckoned to be beyond us. Usually we did boy things like make model aeroplanes or thumb through comics. It was fairly dull. One night in our boredom we came up with a great idea. Men wore hats in those days. There was a tree outside the Balls' house. We tied black cotton to a branch of the tree and pulled it across the pavement and over the fence into the front garden. The plan was to hold it at about hat-height, so that a passer-by would find his headgear whipped off as the cotton caught it. Nobody came by for an eternity. Then we heard strong footsteps in the dark. We were ready. Some unfortunate gent strode past, the cotton caught the crown of his hat and tore it off the back of his head. He stopped and looked up at the tree, peering into the branches, then retrieved his hat. He clamped it on and clumped off. Beside ourselves with fiendish glee – it works, it works – we prepared for our next victim, holding the cotton at what we thought was the right height. Darebin Road was deserted. We waited until we thought we'd had enough. Then, more heavy footsteps. We got ready again. The man walked straight into our trap. But, disaster. He was a soldier in uniform, wearing a slouch hat with chin-strap. As the tightly held cotton caught the hat, it pulled at the strap, which jerked his chin up. 'What the hell,' he said, glaring into the front garden. By now we were scampering across the backyard, over the fence and into the lane. Still, the night had been worth it.

Dad called me into the front room one weekend in second term in 1942. Standing there was Miss Edwards. I knew Miss Edwards. She was a Sunday School teacher who sang solos in the church choir. She had medals for elocution, and used to recite at church concerts.

'Ian,' she said, putting her arms around me, 'your father and I are going to be married, and I want you to be happy in our new family.' Then she planted a moist kiss on my mouth. The world stood still.

I was nearly thirteen. It was almost two years since Mum had died. I'd adjusted to not having a mother. It was okay not having a mother, actually, I thought. You get by. Other people make up for it, like the kids at boarding school and the Balls. Now here's this bombshell. Dad's going to marry Miss Edwards and she'll be my step-mother and I don't care for the idea at all.

I pulled away from her embrace. I looked at Dad and he had a silly half-smile on his face. I said nothing. Like a voice through water I heard Miss Edwards explaining that they were engaged and she supposed it must be a shock for me and that she would love me as if I were her own son because she loved my father so much. Dazed and wordless, I went down the hall to the bedroom, sat on the bed, and my mind went blank. I couldn't think what to think.

Dad had been at the Northcote church for five years, an average length of pastorate, and he'd had 'a call' from the Baptist congregation at St Peter's, an Adelaide suburb. In July, he remarried and we went, the new little family, almost immediately to South Australia, a kind of homecoming for Dad and me.

Dad called his new wife 'Dear' and 'Joyce'. What was I to call her? Since my memory of my own mother was foggy and vague, I couldn't see what else I could call my step-mother other than 'Mum'. So I did. Nevertheless, we tiptoed around each other for about three months.

The St Peter's manse in First Avenue was an archetypal Adelaide villa, built of dressed blocks of Mount Gambier limestone, with a tiled verandah across the front and down the western side. We had three orange trees (unimaginable in wintry Melbourne) down the other side. The verandah across the back had an enclosed bathroom and toilet. From the kitchen you went up a few steps to the breakfast room and downstairs to the cellar, which was always cold and greenly musty. Dad had a study off the front door, and halfway down the central passageway was an arch hung with thick curtains. After dark, I would run down the passage past the curtains because of a fear of what might be lurking there. On the lid of our upright piano stood a simple framed card:

Fear knocked at the door
Faith opened it
And there was no one there.

I thought about this when faced with the darkness of the passage, but never really understood what it meant. My father obviously liked these pithy sayings. Another card stood on one of the bookcases in his study. It bore a round-faced cartoon cherub standing at a desk, and the words: 'If you've nothing to do, don't do it here!'

The unfamiliar Mum was outgoing, cheery and given to laughing. I felt I was being disloyal to my real mother, but I came soon to enjoy this new menage. It was brighter, somehow. Even Dad was less formal and stiff. I began to think life would be all right.

Carey Baptist Grammar had a brother-school in Adelaide, King's College, a Baptist/Congregational school. It was not difficult for Dad to get me in there; it seems that he'd not been forgotten. The headmaster was Bill Oats: Bill – everybody called him Bill, even the boys – was in his alternative-school, A.S. Neill phase. He would later become the famous headmaster of The Friends' School in Hobart. The year round, irrespective of the weather, he wore shorts, open-neck shirt and sandals. I started in third term, cycling to school from home. Bill, who obviously thought I would be having difficulty making adjustments to a stepmother, got me to spend hours each day working with him in the school gardens, where we talked constantly about little or nothing.

I continued the French I'd started at Carey, and began Latin, from a long way behind. But my Arithmetic was really bad news. I didn't know my tables well, couldn't do long division and couldn't even add up accurately; *mental* arithmetic I could not do at all. As my term at King's went on, I made no improvement. Dad would supervise what little Arithmetic homework we had and even set me extra work, but I got no better. At the end of the year my father removed me. This was a *cause du scandale* in the Baptist Union. How could a Baptist minister take his son away from a Baptist school? Because the boy's not learning anything, my father would have retorted.

And so the next year I was enrolled at Norwood High School, a government school not far from King's.

4. Called

I had a good start at Norwood High, helped by two years of French and a term of Latin. The schooling was incredibly competitive. In my class we were seated in rows from front to back, our place determined by our weekly academic score. We had to record the result of every weekly test in our homework book, even a spelling test out of 10. On Thursday nights we would add up the results and record them as a percentage, corrected to the first decimal point, on a blackboard at the rear of the classroom. If you had a bad run and only scored, say, 48.7 per cent, you had to sit down the front and your name was on the rear board for the whole week for all to see, while someone else could bask in the glory of 98.2 and sit up the back. I remember boys in quiet tears week after week.

Our class teacher's name was A.F. Twartz. Next to our room was the chemistry lab, presided over by our science teacher E.N. Pfitzner. Fifty years later I would come across these German names again; this was South Australia with its Lutheran heritage.

The tide of the war was turning. The Tobruk Rats came home to a heroes' welcome; the Dambusters hit the Mohne Dam and the Ruhr flooded; Rome and Paris were liberated; the D-Day invasion stormed the Normandy beaches; the Japanese were being forced back island by island. My father went on the Reserve List, his regular Chaplain-General duties over now.

Dad, possessed of new energy, threw himself into his work with the St Peter's congregation. My new Mum was there, too, being the minister's wife, running the Ladies Guild, helping out in the Sunday School, visiting the sick at home or in hospital. There was in Adelaide, in Australia, even, a kind of Christendom. That needs explaining a little. After the conversion of the Emperor Constantine in 313 AD, it came about by law that the church became identified with the empire. This meant the unifying of the sacred and the secular. The church was society and society was the church. It was something like that in my youth in Adelaide. At Norwood High we had Religious Instruction weekly, Catholics and Protestants separated. I seem to remember, though I can't be sure, that Church of England boys were a third party. I do remember we had a Salvation Army officer take us for a time, so we were probably a non-Conformist group. All of the boys I got to know at school went to church or at least to a Sunday School, whether it was Congregational or Presbyterian or whatever it was.

Most memoirs of growing up in Australia would give the impression that we all grew up Catholic. Brian Lewis's *Sunday at Kooyong Road* is a rare example of a Protestant childhood; far more familiar are Edmund Campion's *Rockchoppers* and Hugh Lunn's *Over the Top with Jim*, where we learn of the violent nuns and the straps of the Christian Brothers, the sodalities and the first communions. It's as though that was the only encompassing religious life to be had. Not true. The non-Conformist denominations placed demands on adherents quite as encompassing as any Roman Catholic parish. We didn't have the pressures at school that the Catholics had, it must be admitted, but our involvement in our churches was intense.

In Dad's church there were about a dozen of us of the same age. On Friday evenings we had a youth club meeting, during which we played harmless games – keepings-off, indoor cricket, draughts – and finished with a devotional segment and a prayer and benediction from whoever had been deputed to look after us for the night (we had no regular leader). What was good about youth club was walking your current girl-friend home and timidly kissing in the shadows at her front gate.

On Saturday afternoons in the summer there was the church cricket team, matches played on pale, straw-coloured grounds with long grass around the boundary. In the winter the girls played netball, which we went to watch, often cheering too loudly. Most Saturday evenings we were invited to another church for a social, not only Baptist churches but sometimes a Church of Christ or a Methodist.

Sunday morning before church was Christian Endeavour, where we became increasingly familiar with Christian language, hearing over and over words like saviour, victory, atonement, glory, sin, repentance, love, judgement, hope, salvation, forgiveness, faith, God, the cross, redemption. I took these words in through the pores of my skin, uncomplainingly. I thought I knew the meaning of judgement. In a vestibule outside the minister's vestry hung a huge framed lithograph called *The Last Judgement*, in which a bearded, seated figure pointed downwards with a dramatic gesture to a great pit, into which was falling a flailing multitude of tortured Hieronymus Bosch figures. Either side of the grand throne on which God (I knew it had to be God) was sitting were serried ranks of white-garbed angels, all smilingly adoring. As for the other words, like atonement and redemption, I had no real idea what they meant, except that they were part of my world, like isosceles and sonnet.

The morning service began at 11 am *on the dot*. We rose as the choir entered first, followed by my father. In strong, ringing tones he would pronounce some invocation, like 'This is the day which the Lord has made; let us rejoice and be glad in it', and while we were still standing, would pray, but briefly. We sat and he announced the first hymn, which we sang lustily, led by the choir, maybe the twelve-year-old Milton's 'Let us with a gladsome mind/Praise the Lord for He is kind', or the German 'Now thank we all our God/with hearts and hands and voices'. Later in the service the choir sang an anthem, most often one from the pen of that prolific Victorian romantic, Caleb Simper. Unusually for a Baptist minister, Dad always had a psalm chanted during the morning service and here the choir was important in giving a lead to the congregation. I always liked the chants: with a frisson of disloyalty, I would find they took me out of the walls of a preaching place into the medieval dimness of some Gothic place of worship.

I began to realise slowly that Dad had a preaching method. Nine times out of ten, I guess, he preached in the morning from an Old Testament text. He preached justice and right dealing, morality under God. In the evenings he preached, nine times out of ten, I guess, from a New Testament text.

Sunday afternoon was Sunday School. Our Sunday School Superintendent (titles were beloved of Christendom) was Mr A.B.L. White. He was the first man I knew who had three initials before his surname. That in itself was impressive, and equally so was the fact that he was a golfer. Nobody else we had ever known played golf. Golf was for the pagan middle-aged wealthy. A.B.L. White taught postmaster-general apprentices and was in fact the national Postmaster-General's Department golfing champion. When I was fifteen he taught me to play golf. Unheard of. A boy playing golf. A.B.L. gave me a bag of old clubs and we would play at North Adelaide in the school holidays. A.B.L. was married but childless. Was I a surrogate?

There was more. A.B.L. was a conjurer who amazed us at Sunday School concerts. He taught me stage tricks. My fairly useless right hand made cards and billiard balls an impossibility, but A.B.L. gave me equipment for illusions at a distance: disappearing glasses of water, knotted wooden rings freed with a tap of the magician's wand. I loved it. I got to be on stage.

Then, a bit like Sarah and Abraham in the Old Testament, A.B.L. White became a father. Golf and magic were henceforth *in my hands*. This gracious, tall man (but inclined to the spherical) then faded from my life. It was good to have known him.

A.B.L. was the superintendent of the Sunday School, not a Sunday School teacher. He took us twice when our regular teacher was away and he was terrific: interesting, informative, knew just how to pitch material, and you wouldn't have played up with him. Our regular teacher was hopeless. Perhaps out of guilt, I have completely suppressed her name. Our class of two girls and four boys had her for three years for our lessons held in the church porch. We teased her unmercifully. When our hilarity at her discomfort reached a certain pitch, she would bow her head and pray for us. We were obviously awful and cruel.

After Sunday School a dozen of us, half girls, half boys, would slope off around the streets of St Peter's, pulling and pushing each other, telling the girls jokes, laughing, showing off, sitting about in a little park. Our parents never expected us home before five o'clock, but never expected us after five, either. If it rained (rats!) we went home straight away.

Our evening service was at seven, again on the dot. Instead of sitting with our parents, as we did in the mornings, the dozen of us sat together in the back row. We passed notes, suppressed giggles and occasionally paid attention to what was going on. Dad's sermons usually came from the gospels, sometimes from the New Testament Letters. Dad commanded attention when he preached and even when we were only half-listening, the incidents in the life of Jesus and the reactions of the minor characters in the drama became fixed in our consciousness. What my father seemed to be on about was response, to what Jesus did and what he said. He never hectored or bullied his listeners: Dad's preaching was always measured and reasonable, firm but not extravagant in style. Even then I knew how carefully he prepared his addresses. He always wrote his sermons out in full, word for word by hand. We never had a typewriter. Then he would transfer sequential phrases to two pages as an *aide-memoire*, clipping these opposing pages into a brown leather cover and underlining key words alternately in red and blue pencil. This meant that Dad never had to turn over pages of text; his notes lay flat on the lectern.

Whatever else we as teenagers thought about our church services, we knew they had dignity. In our better moments we felt shame for our frequent restlessness in the back row.

After church we went off to a sing-song in the home of one of our parents, or another church member's home. We stood around a piano and sang favourite hymns from our Baptist hymnal or from *Alexander's Hymns No.3* – or even, if someone had a copy, from *Sankey's Sacred Songs and Solos*. We sang nineteenth-century evangelical standards like 'Tell me the old, old story', 'I need Thee, every hour', 'Take my life, and let it be/Consecrated, Lord, to Thee' and 'The Old Rugged Cross'. Come nine o'clock, our hostess would produce trays of vanilla slices and lamingtons, and often a couple of tall sponges decorated with strawberries. We had to tuck in quick, for most of us had a curfew of nine-thirty. Often I had to run all the way home to make it on time.

So that was our weekend. Friday night, Saturday afternoon and night, and all day Sunday for almost twelve hours, all under the umbrella of church. No Anglican kids had that sort of experience and, I suspect, very, very few Catholic kids, either. This was our non-Conformist Christendom, sacred and secular as one.

In these days churches of every denomination participated in the on-going ritual of the Harvest Festival. On a given Sunday in Autumn, in our church, the communion table was removed and we erected a long trestle table across the front of the church. A team of women spent hours setting up a display of produce donated by members of the congregation. There were pyramids of apples, of oranges, of tomatoes. There were cauliflowers, huge pumpkins and squash, bunches of parsnips and celery, tumbled piles of potatoes and onions, jars and jars of homemade jams and pickles. Across the back were large sprays and tendrils of vine branches with their brilliant red leaves, and the whole colourful tableau was framed by tall bunches of wheat. In the centre sat a very large loaf of plaited bread and a glass of water.

Just before the children's talk in the service, the Christian Endeavourers came down the front with gifts from home – packets of flour and breakfast cereal, bags of sugar, bottles of tomato sauce – to lay them at the foot of the display. At Harvest Festival we sang lustily (because they had terrific tunes) hymns like

We plough the fields, and scatter
The good seed on the land,
But it is fed and watered
By God's almighty hand

and (my favourite)

Come, ye thankful people, come
Raise the song of harvest home;
All is safely gathered in
Ere the winter storms begin

It never occurred to me that this was a strange ritual to be enacted in a suburban church. We didn't plough and sow and reap – we bought our produce from a shop. I suppose I was vaguely aware that out there in the country people were tending fruit trees, watering cabbages and driving harvesters. But like most suburban worshippers I only really knew my own back garden with its beans, grape vines and almond trees. Nevertheless my friends and I had a keen awareness that God was behind this bounty and that life was all of a piece. Our Harvest Festival reminded us that we should be thankful, and we sang

All good gifts around us
Are sent from heaven above
Then thank the Lord, oh thank the Lord
For all His love.

After the evening service another team got busy packing the vegetables, fruit, jars and packets into cartons to be delivered to children's homes, inner city missions and needy families. I remember we felt good about Harvest Festival, even as teenagers. A sense of gratitude was not strange to us at all. It wasn't *noblesse oblige* or whatever the Australian equivalent of that expression was. We didn't feel superior, just grateful.

We don't have Harvest Festivals any more. That's a pity. Is it because we're not as grateful as we used to be, or because the global economy fills our supermarkets with exotic foodstuffs and we've forgotten the smell of freshly baked crusty bread and the taste of a glass of sweet water, in our case in Adelaide that deliciously sweet tank water?

Outside of church, girls and school, I had one other interest, the Boy Scouts. In my term at King's College I'd joined the Scouts and been away to a camp, which I'd loved. So I became a member of a troop that met weekly near home, and got very involved. I became Patrol Leader of the Kookaburras: I had a left sleeve full of Proficiency Badges – Axemanship, Invalid Cookery, Naturalist and others – and every school holidays for nearly three years went hiking and camping, often with another patrol leader from the same troop called Lee. We'd catch a train into the Adelaide Hills and hike for sometimes five days, carrying all our own gear and food. I'm sure I'm not being sentimental when I say that I found myself becoming ever more and more aware of the complexity of creation during these expeditions. Quite vividly I remember once waking up in my one-man tent on the banks of the Onkaparinga River. As my arm brushed against the tent roof, there was a tinkling as shards of ice slid off. I poked my head out and could see that the grassy meadow where we'd camped was gleaming silver with frost, and a squatting rabbit, five paces off, was staring at me. It was a moment of revelation, of still and breathless beauty. The sacred had broken in.

I enjoyed being a teenager. I think I grew up at the best time in Australia. In the war years in St Peter's, Dad and I dug an air-raid shelter in the back garden. We roofed it with corrugated iron, and dug earthen steps. The first winter rains flooded the floor, then wore away the steps to a steep incline. It was a bit like the air-raid trenches we had at school, along the western boundary fence – they, too, were always full of puddles. I rode to Scouts with my bicycle headlamp blacked out according to Air Raid Warden's advice, and we had blackout curtains on all the windows at home. Mum juggled the ration books with food and clothing coupons. From booklets I became adept at recognising the silhouettes of Luftwaffe aircraft, Junkers and Stukas, and followed the fortunes of war first in Europe and Africa and then in the Pacific. I saw American troops in Rundle Street in freshly dry-cleaned uniforms. I screamed and yelled and danced in King William Street on VE Day and VP Day with the kids from church.

I've read a number of teenage fiction memoirs from *Catcher in the Rye* onwards and begin to wonder if something escaped me as I was growing up. I don't remember ever being suicidally depressed or hating my parents or suffering the agonies of unrequited love. I remember being unjustly treated by a teacher only once.

Our French teacher at Norwood High was an expatriate called Monsieur du Crae. I was the only boy in the Leaving French class. We were translating a Lamartine poem about a gentle, soft day and were stumbling over the word *embaumé*. I cheerfully but seriously suggested 'balmy'. One of the girls giggled. M. du Crae stepped up to my desk, slapped me fiercely across the face and hissed, 'Get out!' I cycled home at lunchtime and told the story. Dad suggested I tell the headmaster. Which I did. I got a story from him of M. du Crae's World War I experiences which had left him at times irrational. Try to understand, I was urged. Next French lesson it was as though nothing had happened. But it had.

We carried our books in tall, oblong kit-bags that fitted conveniently between the handlebars of our bikes. At the end of the day a column of boys would ride home down the gentle incline of Shakespeare Avenue. The greatest wheeze was to draw abreast of somebody you knew and, with a flick of the left wrist, drop your kit-bag under the hapless rider's front wheel. The unwritten rule was that you didn't do it to anyone on the outside – that would be too dangerous. On the inside you simply caused your victim to catapult into the gutter. Very often boys would venture home with their kit bags squashed flat. I would find my friend Lance pedalling beside me, keeping pace and smiling. 'No, please don't! Please!' I would giggle. A sudden hand movement and I grabbed at the brake, but too late. I hit his bag, the frame of the bike slewed to one side and I rolled heavily on my shoulder onto the grass of the narrow nature-strip, laughing. Life was simple.

Another friend, Peter, lived out near Klemzig, then a market-garden area on the outskirts of the eastern suburbs. He'd built a land-yacht. It was big, like a billy-cart for two, and the person 'sailing' it used cords to steer its swivelling front axle. It had a mast about seven feet tall and a square sail made of old bedsheets sewn together. Peter launched it one Saturday afternoon; I felt very privileged to be the only invitee. A southerly was blowing from down the Gulf to the foothills at Magill. As we dragged the craft along a straight bitumen road into the teeth of this wind, we felt like Captain Scott's party on the polar ice – we were doing extracts from Scott's diary in English at school. Having given ourselves about 400 metres, we turned the craft around and hoisted the sail. The yacht bucked and pulled and it was all we could do to hold it steady while we took our seats.

Then we were off. The craft was alive. The sail blew out like a spinnaker and four inches from our bottoms the bitumen raced past in a blur. But Peter had no nautical instincts, and nor had I. Without warning the wind shifted sou-sou-west. It was enough. The spars at top and bottom of the sail swung to our right and at high speed we leapt out of control across the road, hit the gravel and plunged into a deep ditch. The mast snapped with a noise like a gun and Peter went flying one way, I the other. When we scrambled to our feet and looked through the tall grasses, we could see that the craft's back was broken, two of the pram wheels were buckled beyond salvation and the sail was in shreds. We laughed until it hurt. We had travelled about forty metres.

I once took a girl called Norma to the school dance. She had long golden hair that she wore in a plait, and breasts that demanded notice. Norma went to our Sunday School and lived only fifty metres from the manse. The convenience could not have been surpassed. After an evening basking in others' astonishment, I walked her home and prepared to kiss her (and she me, I like to think) when her father opened the front door with 'That you, Norma?' I ran. Safe in my bedroom at home I stole a glance at a magazine photograph of Jane Russell that was pinned on the back of my wardrobe door, and shut it quickly. I could scarcely tell what I was feeling.

I knew what some feelings were. One stifling summer morning I was sitting on the side verandah holding the hose, directing it across the gravel path onto the flower beds by the fence, while at the same time I was reading Edgar Allan Poe's story 'The Black Cat'. The sun stung my face and arms. As I reached the last page, a chill rushed through me. 'Frightened out of his wits' was a phrase I'd heard and now I knew what it meant. In dark terror I looked around me, but there was nothing, nobody. The inert printed page had done this to me, frightened me out of my wits.

The Bills family were very musical members of our church. Mother and two daughters sang in the choir. Son Malcolm appeared very infrequently. When I was fifteen (so much happened when I was fifteen) I was invited alone to a musical evening at their home. I could scarcely have imagined what awaited me. The lid and front had been removed from the upright piano in their sitting room. Seated on dining table chairs, with pages of newspaper at their feet, were a trumpeter, a trombonist, a clarinettist and a tuba player. Next to the piano was a drummer and next to him a banjo player. Malcolm Bills was striking the most delicate chords on the piano and decorating them with what I would later recognise as Jelly Roll Morton's bells. The rest of the band shouted approval when he finished. Then they all played. They began with the traditional '1919 March' and quite swept me away. It was all so relaxed, so vital, so noisy, so cheerful. After each piece the brass players emptied their instruments of saliva over the newspapers. They made rough plans before playing and once or twice broke off and started again. I'd never heard music like it before. This was the period of the big swing bands, Glenn Miller, Tommy Dorsey and the rest, and I whistled their tunes as I rode my bike to school. But this New Orleans-derived jazz was quite something else. And the band that played in the Bills family home was more than merely amateur: the tall trombone player was a Dave Dallwitz who was to become a well-known name in Australian art and traditional jazz circles. The hook was in my mouth and I could never be rid of it. I went again to these mid-week sessions, and again.

Traditional jazz became a small but intense part of me, sometimes tucked away, but responded to for ten, twenty, forty, fifty years and more. I came to know the playing of 'Kid' Ory, Johnny Dodds, Cripple Clarence Lofton, George Lewis and Omer Simeon, Albert Ammons and Meade Lux Lewis, the young Louis Armstrong, Sidney Bechet. I bought books on jazz, collected records on scratchy, obscure 78 rpm vinyl labels, once ordered from America two recordings of the members of the Zenith Brass Band, whose average age at the time of recording was seventy-two: they had been marching in the streets of New Orleans before World War I. I knew enough to recognise that a number of Australian bands had the temperament to enable them to reproduce the angst-free rhythms and melodies of the black bands: Dave Dallwitz could do it, and pianist Graeme Bell (I had the rare and complete set of his first Regal Zonaphone recordings) and the very Melbourne-sounding Len Barnard and a young Frank Traynor. My frustration was that I couldn't myself play. The atrophied thumb had left my right hand an almost useless liability, so I never learned the piano or any musical instrument. All I could do was to tell people about jazz. When later I became a teacher, I left behind a jazz appreciation society in every school I taught at. In one, I played washboard in a boys' band that was an offshoot of our jazz club. In another I helped encourage the fledgling Red Onions Jazz Band, a group that became known internationally.

This introduction to jazz at the Bills's house was a corollary, additional to my mainstream experience of the church. I'd come to be part of it, like breathing. For example, I'd been going to Christian Endeavour rallies for what seemed years. These were encouraging gatherings. Most CE groups had just eight or a dozen members except in very large churches, and we often felt pretty lonely. But the great metropolitan rallies pulled in four or five hundred Endeavourers every month. From the rallies we gained a sense that we were part of a large and vital movement. They were usually held in capacious inner-city churches mostly built in the nineteenth century. On Saturday night great crowds of teenagers milled about on city pavements, spilling out onto the streets. Inside, we were squeezed into pews, and chairs appeared down the aisles. In such a multitude our inhibitions faded and we bellowed, 'And can it be that I should gain/An interest in the Saviour's blood?' and 'There is no love like the love of Jesus/ Never to fail or fall'. During the service young people would give 'testimonies' (the word had a special significance for Christian Endeavourers) and tell the throng, often falteringly and inarticulately, how the Lord Jesus had come into their lives and changed them forever. Missionaries on furlough would tell us how the Lord had sustained them in deserts or jungles and was doing a mighty work among the heathen.

More singing, and the evangelist would preach. He holds a large, floppy, black Bible in one hand – the Word, the Sword of the Spirit – and frequently consults it, flipping over the rice-paper pages as he darts from 1 Peter 2:24 to Isaiah 53:6 to John 1:12, or whatever texts suit his theme. He preaches with vigour for half an hour, judiciously inserting amusing anecdotes at which the hundreds of us laugh loudly, for doesn't this show that we Christians are not glum but have the glory, have been given the 'life more abundant'?

Then the preacher works to his climax, which is 'the appeal'. He urges us to receive the Lord Jesus into our hearts, to give ourselves to Him in total surrender. We're not to consider ourselves unworthy, for the Lord is sufficient for us. The preacher asks us just to bow our heads in prayer, and he pleads for those convicted of sin and in need of salvation to 'come forward' (another phrase of special significance). We roll our eyes up in our bowed heads to see how many are going forward to commit themselves to Jesus: one, two, half a dozen, sometimes someone we know.

The organ begins to play softly. The preacher renews his invitation and the knot of young people at the foot of the pulpit grows. Where we sit we begin to sing. Perhaps it's

I am trusting Thee, Lord Jesus,
Trusting only Thee,
Trusting Thee for full salvation,
Great and free.

or perhaps

Just as I am – without one plea,
But that Thy blood was shed for me,
And that Thou bidd'st me come to Thee,
O Lamb of God, I come.

Now the preacher extends the appeal. Between verses of the hymn, he asks for those in need of reconsecration to come forward. By hymn's end there are twenty or thirty people down there with 'workers' (whose task it is to counsel the converts) quietly moving in among them. As those who've gone forward file out to the back of the church to sign their decision cards and be prayed over, we rise to sing a concluding hymn.

I knew all this stuff. Not that my father ever harped on about the chains of sin or the blood of the Lamb, for it was not his language, but osmotically it was part of me. I sat through appeal after appeal. I had no needs. I knew it all.

Then one mid-winter night it all changed. I was almost sixteen. I was at yet another CE rally, by a curious chance being held in Adelaide's Central Baptist Church in Flinders Street. I was sitting on the left-hand side, squashed up against the kids from our Intermediate Christian Endeavour group. The preacher's theme was that you must never let anyone persuade you that the church is finished.

I remember the story that he skilfully used to break the tension of his address. 'There was once a young man,' he told us confidentially, 'who lived in a little town on the River Murray. He worked here in town, and had been home for the weekend to see his family. On the Sunday morning he was walking to the punt and as he came over the rise of the river bank, he saw the punt two yards out in the water. "Oh, gosh," he said to himself, "I'm late!" He raced down the roadway to the river's edge, hurled his bag across the water to land on the deck of the punt, ran back up the roadway a little, and sprinted down at great speed. He launched himself into a flying leap, his feet touched the metal flange of the punt and his hands grabbed the top of the wire gate. He'd made it. The punt operator roared at him from a corrugated-iron shed. "What'd ya do that for?" "I thought I was going to miss it," the young man gasped. "The punt's not going out, ya fool," yelled the operator, "It's just coming in."'

We all laughed in genuine amusement. The preacher waited until the great church was silent again, leaned across the pulpit, and, with the assurance of a professional actor, whispered, 'The church isn't going out: it's just coming in.' The metaphor struck me as very apt. I thought of cold evening services when my father preached to a congregation of barely thirty hardy souls. I used to wonder about that. Perhaps I was not getting it right.

I was reflecting on this when I became aware of a golden glow up in the south-eastern corner of the church. I can't claim it was in the form of something or someone recognisable. I could have wished it was Jesus beckoning me, but it wasn't. It was just something. I want to call it a religious experience – it was extra-corporeal, at least, and that was enough. When the preacher made his appeal I went forward, astonishing the kids from our church as I clambered over their knees. Out the back I signed a decision card which read

Relying on the Holy Spirit, I turn to God
from my sin, I accept Jesus Christ as my
Saviour, I resolve to confess Him as Lord.

The following morning, Sunday, I squeezed passed my father on the way to the toilet. He was shaving in the bathroom.

'You were late home last night,' he said.

'Yes, Dad, I went forward at the rally.'

I thought he'd be terribly pleased.

'Do you know what you've done?' he asked calmly.

I couldn't believe it. Here's my father, a minister of the Gospel, and I tell him I've accepted Jesus Christ as my Personal Saviour and all he does is ask if I know what I've done.

'Yes, I think so,' I replied rather haughtily.

5. 'Jesus Wants Me … For a Sunbeam'?

I was a Christian by profession now. What did the Lord want of me? How could I serve Him? For my part I had no doubt. I'd become a minister, like Dad. Well, not *like* Dad. I'd be more relaxed. I liked the idea of preaching the Word from a pulpit. I'd make a good preacher, I thought.

Dad asked me if I wanted to be baptised, and of course I said yes to that very public witness to my new-found faith. One Sunday evening, dressed in white cricket pants and a white shirt, I stepped down into the tepid water of our open baptistry to meet my father. Dad was waiting in waders and a preaching gown weighted at the hem. He asked me if I accepted Jesus Christ as my Saviour, I said yes, and in the name of the Father, Son and Holy Ghost he plunged me beneath the water and as I rose (into newness of life was the theology of it), the whole congregation burst into the singing of 'Follow, follow, I will follow Jesus …' I think back now and wonder what was going through my father's head. Adult baptism was the great sacrament of Baptist believers. Here he was baptising his own son. Surely he felt some tremor of emotion? 'Good, son,' was all he said when we got home that night.

Feeling I must have him on side, I told Dad that week I wanted to be a minister. He was unimpressed. That's all very well and noble, he said, but too many men go into the ministry without experience of life. Do something else into your twenties and then see if you still want to be a preacher.

What? I'd only ever thought of two things, joining the army or becoming a commercial artist, because I'd always enjoyed drawing and doodling designs. Teaching, Dad said, what about teaching? I'd never in my wildest dreams thought of being a teacher. Why not get a student bursary (he'd obviously sussed it all out), go to the university, teach for three years, and then see if you're interested in the ministry. So that was that. I got a bursary and had to go to Adelaide High for a Leaving Honours year.

There always seemed to be something tweaking at my beliefs and religious practices. At Adelaide High once a week the senior forms trooped over the road to the Grote Street Church of Christ for Religious Instruction. The minister who took the period was the Presbyterian Very Reverend J.R. Blanchard, BA. He was good. I liked what he said, and as an enthusiastic young Christian I paid close attention. But one aspect astounded me: he *read* his prayers. He wrote them out and read them! This was quite beyond my experience. Baptist prayers in church were extempore: somehow you knew what to say. Dad always prayed like that. I'm sure he thought in advance who or what he'd pray for – Mrs Watkins in hospital, or the victims of an earthquake in Peru – but he would never have written out a prayer. But I had to admit that the Very Reverend J.R. Blanchard's prayers *sounded* so well. The language was honed, there were no stumblings or pauses. They were of a piece with his written-out and crafted addresses to us.

Next year I went to the Adelaide Teachers' College in the city's Kintore Avenue and was enrolled in the first year of an Arts degree at Adelaide University. *That* pleased Dad.

It was a good time to be at the Teachers' College, partly thanks to the ex-servicemen who were entering under the Commonwealth Reconstruction Training Scheme. These

CRTS students were older than those of us straight from school, and often had endured horrendous experiences that had matured them beyond their years. I picked up friends in my age group but also had among my intimates CRTS men like Col Wood (ex-Navy) and Bill Dickson (ex-RAAF).

Bill was intending to go to Croker Island off Arnhem Land as a teacher-missionary. I thought this might be something for me, and I even took a term's course in blacksmithing at Thebarton Tech because Bill thought it might come in handy. The Aboriginal mission idea soon faded, however. Life in college and at university was too seductive.

I became a reporter and poet on the university newspaper *On Dit* and did the same job with the college news sheet. I had poems published in the college magazine, *Torch,* and the university magazine, *Phoenix*, and won the university's Bundey Prize for English verse. I really thought I'd become a poet. I wrote regularly, structured and free verse, I was always experimenting. It went back, I suppose, to the only child telling stories to Teddy and Dolly, to the daydreams in my polio splint and to a wonderfully demanding English teacher at Norwood High, who published me in the school magazine. I won US$50 in a poetry competition in an American religious magazine. When in the early 1960s the Australian Broadcasting Commission announced a competition, I decided to give it a go. The poem was to last thirty minutes' broadcast time and be accessible on a first hearing. I wrote what I termed 'a poem for voices' about the explorer Charles Sturt's search for an island sea. In 'The Captain and the Birds' I tried to hold the different characters' voices together by means of references to the birds Sturt observed on his fruitless journey. The first prize in the competition went to Dorothy Hewett, then a well-known poet and now a *grande dame* of Australian literature. I was awarded the second prize. After 'The Captain and the Birds' was broadcast with some wonderfully professional acting, John Thompson, poet, ABC producer and judge of the competition, was recklessly honest enough to ring me to say that if they'd only delayed their decision until after they had heard a recording of the poems, the award would have come to me. Remembering that phone call still gives me a warm glow.

At teachers' college I appeared in plays and revues. One year I played Major-General Stanley in *The Pirates of Penzance*. I still have a newspaper cutting that reads, 'Ian Hansen, who has the role of the major-general, is a versatile young man. I've seen him, in order, as a conjurer, comedian and in the cast of an Eric Linklater play.' I was, in fact, a show-off. I sang in the college's chamber choir, the Domine Singers, and went on country tours with them.

I had girlfriends. This afforded Mum much amusement – not that my having them was funny, but that I fell so helplessly in love with them. They were, of course, church girls. What other sort were there? Not all of them were Baptists; some were Methodist, or Presbyterian or Church of Christ. Never a Congregationalist, at least that I can remember. Once, by mistake, an atheist.

After five years at St Peters, with its leafy streets and its middle class air, it was time for Dad to move on. During the year I went to teachers' college and university he received a call from the congregation at the West Croydon church. In the early 1920s when Dad had been minister at the Hindmarsh church, he had been instrumental in establishing a 'cause', as it was called then, in West Croydon. The cause had prospered and become a church in its own right. Now, in a sense, he was coming home to his first pastorate, with its factory roofs and its working class style.

The manse and the church were just off the Port Road, the

main artery between the city centre and the wharves of Port Adelaide. There was a bike-track down the Port Road, and that was my way to the university. I rode that arrow-straight bike track (no gears: they were pretty rare in those days) in wind and rain, on glaring summer afternoons, on sharp, frosty mornings. Never complained. Never thought to complain. Who of my age ever had a car, or a motor-bike even? Few. You could get a driver's licence at sixteen on the strength of a written test. I had a licence and rode friends' motor-bikes, a little 250 cc Triumph and a Matchless 500, but most times it was pedalling for me.

Dad and Mum seemed happier at West Croydon, though I can't tell you why. Did something go wrong at St Peter's? With the deacons, perhaps? Dad kept a lot of his books in the St Peter's vestry, and I remember him telling me that one of the deacons had remarked unfavourably on the number of books he spied by Leslie Weatherhead and H.E. Fosdick, renegade religious commentators of that time. At all events, our new congregation was welcoming. Mum was especially bouncy. We had developed this genuine relationship in which she'd become a mother, my mother. I reckoned step-mothers only got a bad press in fairy tales: mine was all right. The two of us always did the dishes together in the evenings if I was home. We joked and threw soap suds or tea towels at each other. She would take my part if she thought Dad was being too demanding. I liked that.

I was leading a kind of double life. Despite all my worldly activities, the acting, the singing, I maintained a witness of a kind among my evangelical friends. For that's what I'd become by default: an evangelical. To us, the Student Christian Movement was very suspect. Its members were not 'sound'. They were inclined to hold committee meetings without prayer, we heard, and their business seemed to be quasi-political, dealing with aid to overseas countries instead of winning souls for Christ here in Adelaide. Our place was with the Evangelical Union. It was a source of anguish for me not being able to get to the early morning prayer meetings of EU, but often I was tired from rehearsals the previous night. When I was able to attend, I heard what I later called the 'just and really' style of praying. The EU prayers were extempore, of course, no Blanchard preciseness here. They would go like this: 'Our dear Lord Jesus, we just pray that you will come to us this morning and really bless us here. Jesus, just vouchsafe your presence to us, for we are really in need of your grace and forgiveness. Just hear us, Lord Jesus, just come, Jesus, Lord, and really enter our hearts as we pray together here'. To my surprise I found these prayers vaguely distasteful, even grating. But these were my brothers and sisters in Christ, so I allowed myself to get used to it. I even slipped into the style myself when emotionally fraught.

We were a tight little community, we who had the burden of souls upon us. I found myself somehow involved with a group of workers for the Campaigners for Christ movement. They had set up a large room on the first floor of a building opposite the Adelaide Railway Station as a lounge with provisions for serving hot snacks. The idea was for us who professed the Lord Jesus (how the language comes back to me) to bring to the lounge friends and acquaintances who didn't know the Lord, so we could counsel them by taking them through the Scriptures. I had a New Testament with key salvation verses printed in red under sections marked in the margin like 'Coming to Christ', 'Comfort in sorrow' and 'Guidance and leading'. I don't remember any time when I was there counselling an unbeliever or backslider. Usually we sat, two or three of us, discussing among ourselves texts like

Romans 3:9,10 – 'We have before proved both Jews and Gentiles, that they are all under sin; as it is written, There is none righteous, no, not one' – and Thessalonians 5,5: 'But ye, brethren, are not in darkness, that that day should overtake you as a thief'. The intensity of our analysis of God's Word was astounding. There was, however, one issue that came up often. We were trying to discern the Will of God.

What it meant for us then was simple. God had a plan for all of us. If it was His will, we simply accepted it, because of the higher purpose behind the will. If one of us had failed, say, a final exam in History II, despite our praying for success, then God was telling us something. He wasn't telling us we hadn't worked hard enough; he was telling us that we were, say, beginning to think more highly of ourselves than we ought, and needed to be made humble. Or if a friend was stricken with a painful illness, then God was thereby offering that friend the opportunity to demonstrate courage in adversity and purification of the soul. God, we argued among ourselves, was interested in each of us in the most intimate way. He guided all our decisions because His will was for us. Everything that happened was the will of God.

This, of course, was nonsense, I later realised. The first mistake we made, and we were reasonably intelligent university undergraduates, was that we never attempted to *define* the will of God. The phrase was, itself, a kind of fatalism, a kind of talisman, a Christian phylactery, a kind of charm against the evil of the world. We never really asked ourselves what it was.

I could tell that earnest little group now what I believe the will of God to be. For it is possible to see three aspects here. There's first of all what we might call the intentional will of God. That means the way in which God pours out himself in goodness (with great insight Graham Greene wrote of 'the incredible possibility of God'). Goodness is what God intends and therefore we have to dissociate from the 'will of God' phrase all that is evil, unpleasant and stressful. What sort of God would it be who, of his own intention, poured out misery, unhappiness, bereavement, calamity and ill-health upon the children of his creation and then would ask them to say through their tears, 'Thy will be done'? We have to break completely with the idea that everything that happens is the will of God in the sense of being his intention. It's not God's intention that an eight-year-old in a children's hospital should suffer the agony of an incurable cancer. It's not God's intention that a family should live day by day with grief and anger. It's not God's intention that a teenager should die of a heroin overdose slumped against a wall in a city lane. What we have to come to terms with is the idea that the intentional will of God can be defeated by the will of men and women *for the time being*.

The will of the Indonesian militarists in the 1980s and 1990s was defeating the will of God for peace in East Timor *for a time*. It certainly wasn't God's will that thousands should die in that conflict. For some people, the phrase 'the will of God' becomes like a mantra, an incantation to protect them against really facing the truth. Some people get a lot of comfort supposing their tragedies are the will of God: it helps them to cope, somehow, but they're finally living a lie. There's another popular argument, too. Some of the finest qualities in people are forged in the 'crucible of suffering' (a pompous expression) and therefore suffering is part of the will of God. But pain of itself doesn't make people noble: the nobility was always there and the pain and suffering merely gave it expression. To say of anguish and fear and disease that it's the will of God is a blasphemy. Such terrors have no part in the intentional will of God.

There is a second aspect, which we may call the circumstantial will of God. For people who believe in God anyway, there is a plan for them in certain circumstances. There may be an intentional purpose of God for our lives, but, because of humankind's free will, circumstances are created that cut across God's plans. This circumstantial will is as it were within the will of God, in that if we accept it and do it, then our minds can feel a stillness through which to express the ideal plan of God. As a child I wondered whether the circumstances of my polio were a punishment from God, and my Campaigners for Christ colleagues had a primitive view not far removed from that. Instead, I somehow got hold of my circumstances and wrestled something from them. I believe now that no possible situation can ever arise which of itself has the power either to defeat me or to defeat what I call God.

There's a third element in the will of God. This I call God's ultimate will. The ultimate will of God is for men and women to recover a unity with him, but it is too early in this memoir to explore this. Later.

I don't imagine that any of this would have gone down at all well in that first floor lounge opposite the railway station. Over the doorway to Carl Jung's house in Kusnacht were the words *Vocatus atque non vocatus, Deus aderit* – Called and not called, God will be here. For Jung, that was a basic truth. Whether you call God, want God or not, he'll come anyway, he'll be there. Jung reckoned that submission to the will of God was the ultimate task in the whole process of individuation, of becoming oneself. To follow God's will should be a freeing experience, Paul said, and we have it in the words of the Book of Common Prayer; 'God in whose service is perfect freedom'. *That* was the trouble with us in our closed little evangelical group. We weren't free. We were hemmed in by all sorts of strictures that had nothing to do with love or freedom. Even to conceive of God's will in the terms I have just described is to find oneself often on the edge. We EUers and Campaigners lacked the courage to go to the edge.

We were keen. We stood on street corners along the city's North Terrace and on the sea-front at Glenelg and spoke the words the Lord had given us to say. We harangued passersby, preaching loudly of sin and the cleansing power of Jesus' blood, of the judgement to come to those who resisted the winsome call of Jesus. This was our witness to the unwashed. Nobody stopped to listen, as I recall, but we went on all the same, for we were called to proclaim the gospel of our Lord Jesus Christ. We recognised dimly that we were a subculture of the Christian church, but such was our religious and spiritual arrogance that we believed it to be the will of God that we should engage in street evangelism, and speak the word of the Lord to anyone we came in contact with, even in a railway carriage. Didn't the Scriptures tell us that the time was nigh?

One fact I learned from the Campaigners for Christ people stuck with me. One of their salaried workers told us about the fish symbol in the early church. Remarkably, this was fifty years before the symbol began appearing in the rear windows of cars. Anyway, he described the simple two lines, one concave, one convex, in the shape of a fish from nose to tail. The word for fish in Greek was *ichthus*, and it was made up from the initial letters (in Greek) of the phrase, 'Jesus Christ, Son of God, Saviour'. This abstraction of the fish-shape was used by the early Christians to indicate the way to places of worship: 'It was a secret clue for believers. It was dangerous to believe, and drawing the picture in the dust while in conversation was a gesture of solidarity.' All of this impressed me. I'd never heard it before. It appealed,

I suppose, because it was a symbol, a metaphor, an expression of a deep significance. The fish-idea became a part of my belief system. Doodling during a lecture, I would find myself drawing these fishes down the margin of my writing pad. The fish came to represent what I put so much store by. It was a visual poem.

One year an American evangelist, Hyman Appelman, visited Australia. He preached in every capital city and was booked into Adelaide's Princess Theatre for a season of four nights. Four of us EUers, who had sung together for fun, were recommended by the Campaigners for Christ workers to the Appelman entourage. We could be a local contribution to the mission. American evangelists always had a songleader to warm up the audience and to conduct their singing. We prepared a hymn (I forget which) in four parts and sang it for Hyman Appelman's songleader, who'd come over a couple of days early from Melbourne to check arrangements. He thought we would do, and arranged that on each of the four nights we would present a different gospel hymn as a male quartet. Because we were doing this for the Lord, we worked hard at it, rehearsing by the hour. Each night we got to the theatre early, loosening up in one of the dressing rooms and running through the hymn. In our pauses we could hear faintly the mission's pianist, out on stage at a grand, doing *his* practice. He was a local, like us, called in. He was the archetypal evangelical rally piano player, the kind that was noisy, thunderous, decorating the hymn tunes with clattering chromatic scales. The song leader loved him. And he seemed to approve of us, even. He would always ' introdooce us' as 'our very own barber-shop quartet'. All he wanted was for us to sing a 'garspel hymn' that would set the mood for the evangelist's message. I can remember only two that we sang, but I remember with absolute clarity those two. One was

In loving kindness Jesus came,
My soul in mercy to reclaim,
And from the depths of sin and shame,
Thro' grace He lifted me!

and continuing for four verses (most of these gospel hymns seemed to have four verses), with the refrain

From sinking sand He lifted me;
With tender hand He lifted me;
From shades of night to plains of light,
Oh, praise His name, he lifted me.

The other was

Softly and tenderly Jesus is calling,
Calling for you and for me,
See on the portals He's waiting and watching,
Watching for you and for me,

with its four-part chorus

Come home, come home,
Ye who are weary, come home,
Earnestly, tenderly, Jesus is calling,
Calling, O sinner, come home!

It never occurred to me that the language of these hymns was tautly sentimental. The darkness of sin, the light from the saving grace of Jesus, the soft call of the Saviour to the weary sinner, these images were part of our evangelical dialect. We spoke a kind of religious patois, an argot that marked us off as chosen. We were on the Lord's side.

I'd been to missions conducted by local evangelists and knew the form and shape of these evening meetings. There were hymns from a hymn sheet (PLEASE DO NOT TAKE AWAY), a lengthy Bible reading, more hymns, a solo from the songleader and the climax was the message. If I'd thought the missions I'd been to were rousing, I was wrong. *This* was rousing. The songleader had extraordinary energy and a voice that had no need of a microphone. He had a repertoire of anecdotes and jokes and delivered them with the flair of a Manhattan stand-up comic. It was thoroughly professional. But the preacher . . .

Hyman Appelman dressed in a pale grey three-piece suit with wide lapels. His ties (a different one each night) were in execrable taste, but glaringly bright. His full face was florid, his greying hair slicked down. At the lectern he was broad and strong, and his baritone voice had a range and a warmth that were, well, seductive.

He needed no notes as he spoke with confident authority. He played with the audience like a skilful actor, roaring at them, whispering, smiling, frowning, pacing to and fro, snatching his big black Bible from the lectern and thumbing through it for a text. Perspiration poured down his face and spun off in a fine shower as his gestures became more vehement.

So he worked his way to his climax: 'Won't you come right down the front here and give your heart to Jeesus? He is calling you from the cross, calling, calling. Can you hear Him? Won't you just open your whole self to his glorious presence?'

Each night we entered the theatre by the side door, proceeding down a side aisle and across the stage to our dressing room out the back. Each night, from the corner of my eye, I could see Hyman Appelman kneeling in intense prayer at a chair off stage to the side. He prayed there probably for half an hour before the service began. On our third night we went backstage a couple of minutes early. As we stood there waiting, I noticed Hyman Appelman was still kneeling in prayer. And then it struck me like a slap across the face. *He was wearing built-up shoes!*

At that moment I became sceptical for the first time in my life. All that I'd put my trust in became confused, insubstantial. This spokesman for the Lord, this preacher of the Word of God, was a sham, a cheat, was vain.

From that revelatory moment things could never be quite the same again.

6. The Making of a Sceptic

Like all generations of Australian males, mine held sport high. I was at a disadvantage in that I couldn't play. Or rather, I couldn't play well, which was in some ways worse. At school I played in B-teams in cricket and football, often as twelfth or nineteenth man. At teachers' college I managed several games with the football team, but that was only during vacations when half the team went to the country for the holidays. It looked as though I'd never be good at sport, and it worried me. As that acute observer of Australian mores, Donald Horne, has said: 'To play sport, or to watch others play, and to read and talk about it is to uphold the nation and build its character.' Standing on the boundary in the rain in football gear and clutching an overcoat around me, waiting for a team-mate to come off injured, I wasn't even upholding my mates, let alone the nation.

My college secondary teaching course was of four years' duration. I completed my BA in the minimum time and therefore had a slack fourth year. To fill up my timetable I did some honours subjects in English and discovered in the university's Dip Phys Ed course a mid-year term's unit called 'Combative Exercises'. Half the unit was wrestling and the second half was boxing. Wrestling was hopeless. I couldn't grab and hold with my right hand; I'd get my opponent off-balance but couldn't snatch at his upper arm to complete the throw. But boxing was different. For my weight I was tall and had a long reach. I had an orthodox stance which meant I led with my left hand. I didn't smoke or drink and, thanks to cycling and hiking, I was pretty fit. At the end of term our teacher, a still active professional boxer, said I should keep it up. Since I lived in West Croydon, he would recommend me to Charlie Mitchell's gym.

I presented myself to Charlie a week later. I already knew about him: he'd been a sparring-partner for the great Les Darcy, world middleweight contender. It struck me how soft-spoken was this one-time Australian champion, with his fuzz of ginger hair and his soft gestures. Two large signs adorned the little gym at the bottom of Charlie's back garden: NO SWEARING and SWEARING NOT ALLOWED.

For three years I trained with Charlie. I kept improving, moved quite fast, had this long reach. Will you enter me for the amateur titles, Charlie? Not quite ready, son, not quite ready. Charlie's boys never lost a bout and I wasn't quite ready, son. Then, in 1953, Charlie entered me as a novice. I was chuffed.

In my three years of waiting, I'd gone often to the school where I now taught with a split lip or a black eye. One night about a fortnight before the championships were to begin, I was working hard on the heavy bag – in close, hooking with both hands – when I felt a jab of pain in my left wrist. It turned out I'd broken a small bone (I suppose today it'd be called a stress fracture) and wouldn't be able to use the hand for over a month. My one good hand. I couldn't run the risk of any permanent damage to it, and so that was the end of my boxing career. I thanked Charlie for being a good teacher, and Mrs Mitchell, a long-suffering stalwart of the local Methodist Church (I couldn't get away from the church) and never went back.

I often wondered why I enjoyed boxing so much. Didn't I believe that 'Blessed are the meek', 'Blessed are the peace-makers', 'Blessed are the merciful'? And how about 'who-soever shall smite thee on thy right cheek, turn to him the other also'? I weaved and ducked around the ring each week, thudding a right hook into my partner's ribs, following up with a left cross to the head. Blood ran from my nose into my mouth, my sparring helmet grew sweaty, I wanted to land one good punch before the three minute bell. And I read my Bible and prayed to the Lord Jesus. It didn't make sense but it felt all right.

I see now that boxing was a wonderfully liberating experience. It was a vent for the escape of a well of deep anger. I was angry about my polio legacy, I was angry at my natural mother for dying when I really needed her, most of all I was angry at my father because I never seemed to be able to please him. The aggression I needed to survive those weekly three-round bouts with Charlie relieved the pressure I didn't know had built up inside me.

I went straight from college and university to teach at Adelaide Boys' High School in its new and rather swanky premises on West Terrace. I had a great time there. I ran a bush walking club with senior boys and (of course) a boxing club and, with the extraordinary George Williams as head producer, was involved in classy productions of *The Merchant of Venice*, *Julius Caesar* and *Hamlet*. ABHS was a tight ship. Our Captain Bligh was A.E. Dinning. At morning recess six hundred boys would gather in the quadrangle, making an immense din. But when Alf Dinning entered the quadrangle on his way to the tuckshop to order lunch, a hush descended on the boys. They stopped pushing and yelling as this ruddy-faced martinet passed through them. By a terrible force of autocratic personality, Alf daily cowed a melee of hundreds.

Few of us on the staff had ever seen Alf smile. His greetings to us in the corridors were always gruff. He was tough on boys, tough on their parents and tough on us. He was also known to be a prominent Methodist layman. A dear and gentle old colleague of mine was a member of the Salvation Army. One day when we were discussing Alf's latest severity, he whispered to me: 'Do you think he's lost the glory?' I've been ever grateful to Dave for that expression. It's served me well whenever I've reflected on some churchman's untoward behaviour.

My enthusiasm for personal evangelism and the language that goes with it was waning. When Alf – the Sacred River we used to call him, from a line in Coleridge's 'Kubla Khan' – asked me to meet with a representative of the Crusader Movement (a kind of EU for schools), I found the earnest workers' turn of phrase too difficult to cope with. Asked if I would act as a mentor to the fledgling group, I said no. But my concern for spreading the faith had not left me. The image of myself as an ordained minister of religion slowly faded, to be replaced by a more amateur view of mission. I came to believe that I could better witness for my Lord (I couldn't quite shake off the jargon) by being the best classroom teacher I could be, and being ready as counsellor as well as transmitter of knowledge.

In my second year at ABHS, we used a conservative poetry anthology called *Poems Old and New*. With our third year classes we did 'The Solitary Reaper', 'Drake's Drum', 'On first looking into Chapman's Homer', 'The Tiger', all that stuff. Approaching Easter, I chose to give my class G.K. Chesterton's 'The Donkey'. *And they didn't get it!* The last stanza

Fools! For I also had my hour;
One far fierce hour and sweet:
There was a shout about my ears,
And palms before my feet

went straight past about two-thirds of the class. So there I was, trying with the help of the boys who had church and Sunday School connections to explain the passion story that followed the entry of Christ into Jerusalem. Perhaps twenty boys in that class had no real understanding of the background to the Easter period, except that it was a holiday from school. If ever I needed convincing that I'd chosen the right job, it was just that experience that did it.

Why, I thought, do we send missionaries from Australia to the uttermost parts of the world to tell the story of Jesus, and there's kids here who know nothing of it? It is part of their cultural inheritance, I argued to myself, and if it needs explaining, I'll explain it. My EU and Campaigners for Christ friends used the expression 'full-time service' to describe people who'd taken up an evangelical career like a preaching missionary or nursing on the mission field. Even then it struck me as an odd expression. If belief meant anything, it coloured the whole of your existence no matter what your career. If you believed at all with any sincerity, then that required full-time commitment.

I loved it in the classroom, partly because I could show off and get paid for it. I was having little success with girls. Whenever I took up with one, I began to picture marriage and family, a romantic response more stereotypically to be expected from the girl than from me. I wanted a family different from the one I remembered as a small child. I'd like to be a father, I thought, different from the one mine had been. My peers at church and school were getting engaged or married, and at twenty-three I seemed to have no prospects. Those nights I'd helped my dancing partners through the window of the nurses' home on North Terrace were over, it appeared.

Every Sunday evening Mum and I would do the dishes

while Dad went over his sermon notes. This night I was moaning to Mum, rattling off the names of friends who'd become engaged or had married. There's just no one for me. Perhaps I'll never marry. Without looking up from the sink, Mum said, 'What about Dorothy?'

'Dorothy who?'

'Our Dorothy,' she said, throwing me a glance.

Before Dad and my new Mum had married, Mum's brother, Ron, had been Dad's Church Treasurer at Northcote. When Ron had married a woman named Jen, Mum had gone to live with them. Dorothy, the first-born and only girl, was followed by three brothers. As the house filled, Dorothy later shared a room with Mum. In a sense, her Auntie Joyce – who became my Mum – had more to do with Dorothy's upbringing than her own mother, busy as Jen was with her small boys. Probably no one knew Dorothy better than Auntie Joyce. On my father's re-marriage, Ron and Jen became my step-uncle and step-aunt, and Dorothy and the boys my step-cousins. I knew them all well. I knew Dorothy was an accomplished pianist, a research librarian and . . .

I would have to think about this.

I didn't have long to think as it turned out. Within a year of the washing-up conversation, Mum was dead. Some kind of bungled diagnosis was behind her death, a cerebral tumour that had never been properly assessed. It was sudden. She was forty-seven. On the April day of Mum's funeral, more than three hundred floral tributes arrived at the church. Others obviously loved her as I did.

There was a complication in the middle of all our grief and sorrow. We'd been living in a house which the church rented as a manse, and now the church had begun to build a manse of its own. The lease had run out on the rented manse and the new one wasn't ready, so Dad and I had to find somewhere to live. One of Dad's soul-mates, the Rev. Harry Bunday, lived with his daughter in the large Mile End Baptist manse nearby, and we went there. Dorothy came over from Melbourne for her Auntie Joyce's funeral and stayed with us for a week. I observed her through my grieving. I was beginning to see her differently. There was a kindliness about her I'd not noticed before, a warm pleasantness. We even took to walking together arm in arm. There seemed to be a growing intimacy. She smiled at me with her eyes. She touched me tenderly. We talked a lot, about Mum, all sorts of things.

Some weeks after the funeral, Dad, Harry and I were sitting around the fire one evening chatting about evangelists and their preaching. We were laughing together when Harry challenged me. 'Go and get a Bible,' he said, 'we've got one somewhere. Find me a verse from anywhere, and I'll get you to Jesus and the cross in less than six sentences.' I opened a Bible towards the front, not wanting to make it easy for him with a New Testament verse. Without looking I poked at the page, and read from 1 Chronicles 11:22. 'Benaiah the son of Jehoiada, the son of a valiant man of Kabzeel, who had done many acts; he slew two lion-like men of Moab: he also went down and slew a lion in a pit in a snowy day.'

Without hesitation Harry rose from his armchair, flung his arms wide, and thundered, 'He slew a lion in a pit in a snowy day. As the prophet Isaiah, tells us: "Though your sins be as scarlet, they shall be white as snow". And what can wash your sins as white as snow? Only the blood of Jesus as it flows from the cross on Calvary's hill!'

Harry collapsed giggling into his chair and panted. 'There. I got it in four sentences, only four!' Opposite him my father was guffawing. I'd never heard him laugh like that before.

And I sat with a silly grin on my face. This wholesome cynicism was another revelation.

Dad and I went into the new manse. One of the church ladies, Mrs Gillies, came three days a week to cook, wash, iron and clean; otherwise it was just the two of us. One evening we were sitting either side of the fireplace. I was marking a Latin test or something and Dad was sucking on his pipe. Suddenly he said to me: 'You don't believe Jesus was born in Bethlehem, do you?'

'What do you mean?' I asked, to cover my shock.

'Jesus was probably born in Nazareth, not Bethlehem', he said.

'But what about the Christmas story? The angels, the stable, the wise men, all that?'

'It's all miracle stories and Old Testament prophecy,' he said. 'In any case, what was a Nazarene couple doing seventy miles from home? Would the Romans, of all people, have required a villager to go all that way to fill out a census form in the place where his ancestors were supposed to have lived centuries before? And Mary as a woman wouldn't be required for the census, so why drag her all that way – especially when she was pregnant?'

I was stunned. 'If you really believe this, why don't you tell the church people from the pulpit?'

'Because I wouldn't want to upset them. And what real difference does it make? Does believing or not believing in the shepherds and the heavenly choir make a difference to the way I live, the way I treat people, the way I care for them in their pain? No, son, no.'

'But you've preached on the wise men and the angels and all that!'

'Yes, but I've also used fairy tales, myths and incidents from novels to illustrate what I'm trying to say. What's the difference? I don't have to believe in them as fact to use them helpfully. Do I?'

The impact was like seeing Hyman Appelman's built-up shoes. I sensed this was a turning point. It certainly was in my relationship with my father.

Only once before had he been open with me. It was on the back verandah at St Peter's. I was sitting cleaning the family shoes, my weekly chore. He looked down at me and said, 'Because your mother and I love each other very much, we wanted to have a baby, but it didn't work out and she lost it. Do you know what I mean?' I nodded. 'So she's going to be a bit tired for a few days. We're not telling anybody. All right?'

Now he was being frank again, revealing just a little of himself. He was probably very lonely. But this was a turning point in another sense. I came 'in a moment', 'in the twinkling of an eye' to own a questioning I'd never had before.

I suppose it's true to say that Dad saw his chance. First he gave me his copy of C.J. Cadoux's *The Life of Jesus* to read. Then he pressed on me H.E. Fosdick's *The Modern Use of the Bible* ('especially what he says about miracles'), and finally his well-thumbed and marked copy of R.E. Welsh's *In Relief of Doubt*. With mounting interest and even excitement I read opinions like

> in 'Matthew' the fig-tree withers immediately: in Mark it is found withered when they pass the following morning ... there are ... strong reasons for regarding this incident as a fictitious equivalent in narrative form of the parable of the barren fig-tree.

and

I cannot think of a miracle as intervention in a philosophically conceived cosmic system; and I do not believe that miracles are the suspension or rupture of universal laws.

or

Nor can Esther (in which the name of God never occurs and which contains no religion at all) be compared with Job in Divine illumination: nor Ruth with the Psalms in spiritual elevation. Each has its own place, carries its own lesson. But . . . they vary in quality, tone, moral impulse, and inspiration. We cannot attach the same value to and recognise the same Divine authority in each and every passage indiscriminately among the different books.

These were not books Dad had just come across. He'd had them for years: he'd read *In Relief of Doubt* before he went to World War I. They'd been part of his intellectual equipment since I was a child, since before I'd been born. This amazed me.

I wasn't sure what to make of Dad any more. He was secretive. He kept all this radicalism to himself. He was surely a theological renegade among his Baptist colleagues in South Australia. Or didn't they realise?

The effect on me was both dramatic and calmly satisfying. I'd spent years at university at the craft of literary criticism and was working toward an MA in Australian Literature. I knew about approaching a text, but it had never occurred to me to use the same skills and techniques in reading the Bible. I came to see that the Synoptic gospels didn't harmonise: I recognised that the gospel writers had particular readerships in mind or put their own slant on their accounts of the life of Jesus. Luke's gospel was quite, quite different from 'Matthew's', and they were both different from Mark's.

It would have scandalised and pained my one-time EU and Campaigners for Christ colleagues if I were to suggest to them that the Noah story was myth, but that's where I was now at. If I had told them that a number of the Old Testament narratives were historically unreliable, they would have fallen to praying for me.

I was moving out of an evangelical culture. That culture had been good to me; it had given me a sense of belonging when I needed it. Now, however, I saw there was another way of responding to my religious impulse. I no longer had to be bound in a language or dialect. When I talked religion, I had no longer to use incantatory expressions like 'the blood of our Lord Jesus Christ'. I could use common speech.

Sometimes at home when I was preparing a new lesson series for school or making notes for my thesis, I'd find myself doodling with fish-shapes. Because the symbol was so firmly associated with the hot-house enthusiasms in that room opposite the railway station I would have to deconstruct it, remove from it all pious accretions, pare it back to its essence, undress it. It had become overlaid for many believers with desperate hopes and fears and with on-going anxieties. I'd have to reduce it to those two clean lines. It came to me that I'd begun that process now. It wouldn't be easy.

From earliest childhood I'd been churched. By the time I could think for myself I'd been in thrall to Sunday School and Christian Endeavour. As a teenager I'd taken a stand 'trusting in the Lord Jesus Christ', and had been baptised as a public profession of my faith. I witnessed for my Lord and quoted verse after verse of the scriptural promises. I attended evangelical rallies, missions and meetings, and prayed people into the Kingdom. You might have thought that the dramatic discoveries I had just made would leave me disenchanted with my belief system. I knew preacher's kids who would have given the whole game away. But somehow the disclosure that I couldn't accept Scripture at its face-value seemed not to make a difference to my faith position. I was still a believer.

By now (what am I? Twenty-three years old?) I'm a Sunday School teacher, I write lesson outlines for the Baptists' national teachers' guides, I'm a study group leader at young people's camps, I give amusing addresses at other churches' Sunday School anniversaries. And there's my problem. I'm full of all these exciting ideas about God, Jesus and the resurrection, about the mythical strands in the Old Testament – and I've got to keep quiet about them, I wouldn't want to upset people.

I managed it by avoiding sentimental and pious language, telling stories, conducting studies of Bible passages in a language that was plain and free. But I couldn't escape the feeling that I was being a fraud, like my father. I was reminded of a short story by Graham Greene, called 'I Spy', where a young boy in the act of stealing and cheating overhears his father being arrested as a spy. Well, I said to myself, my father has lived with this holy deception all the years of his pulpit ministry, and I'll probably do the same.

For I recognised that if people knew I had taken on heretical views, that would mean the end of me. I'd never be invited to talk to a youth group or run a study series again. Our church community, the larger Baptist constituency, would write me off. You see, I was still a show-off. I loved being out front. I couldn't bear to lose that. So I kept quiet. I went on as though nothing had happened.

Often in winter when I came home late from a film or meeting, I'd find Dad sitting in front of the fire. There'd be an unread book on the arm of the chair and he'd be staring at the gold and white ash of the mallee roots in the fireplace. He'd be sucking at his pipe, gazing into the fire.

7. Entr'acte

This is a book about what I believe about the world and people and myself, as influenced by what has happened to me – in my autobiography, my self-told tale. I've written it because there's a great gap between books of theology, which few lay people read, and autobiographies, in which faith stances are referred to only in passing, if at all. I'm trying to bridge that gap and to link life-experiences and beliefs.

I'm trying to steer my way between two comparatively recent Australian books, David Marr's *The High Price of Heaven* and David Tacey's *Edge of the Sacred*. Marr's enlarged collection of some of his newspaper articles comes to be an attack on the Church: the writer is embittered as a result of the way the Church let him down when he was an adolescent. So he charges the Church's adherents with being kill-joys, with lacking sensitivity and compassion, with being bullies. I don't intend to castigate the Church or Christians generally, though heaven knows, there are grounds for being critical. Nor do I want to mount a defence of the Church and Christians. I'm not an institutionalist but simply a believer.

On the other hand, I don't intend to explore that recent (it seems) discovery by, first, Catholics and then later by Protestants, of a late-twentieth century spirituality. I have a deep awareness of spirit. Tacey gets it right:

> Embarrassment will arise as we turn to face soul and spirit, which our positivist ethic has taught us to disparage and revile. Soul and spirit are felt to be superstitions of a bygone era, discredited by scientific advancement and rejected by secular society.

It's difficult to maintain a sense of the sacred in an arrogantly secular society like ours. But, and Tacey would agree, this secularism doesn't mean a lack of religious sensibilities, merely widespread bad religion. However, I'm not going to propose any kind of Christian Dreaming here, fascinating though the issue is, both for Tacey and for people like me. I just want to find a middle course.

Near my seventieth birthday I began to wonder why it was that, after over fifty years of fairly committed association with the Christian church, I was still a believer. And I further wondered whether I had anything to confess, really. For it's widely held that anyone over forty-five is past it and has nothing to say or contribute to any debate. But given the wild and dizzying changes in the world over these fifty years, perhaps it's a kind of miracle that anyone could survive at all. I can still remember when I was about four (so that was over sixty-five years ago, but no matter) my father coming home, his face shining, to tell my mother and me he had heard a commentary on a Test Match on the wireless. A neighbour several houses up from ours had invited my father to listen in with earphones to the ball-by-ball description of Australia vs the Poms. My father (I think he was really a closet romantic) was beside himself with the wonder of it. So I've lived from that primitive technology to the World Wide Web (which I understand as little about as my father understood about the wireless). I've seen the old, fixed points of reference fade or disappear: family and home, community, trust, generally accepted moral codes, a generally accepted belief system.

I get frustrated about those people who, when pressed, say, 'I'm not religious, but . . .' and proceed to give an account of some experience that by any assessment I would call 'religious'. It is plain nonsense to deny religiousness. We're all body, mind and spirit. We all have religious apprehensions, from marvelling at a brilliant sunrise to being moved by some act of charity. Religiousness has to do with the capacity to wonder. Some have a greater capacity to wonder than others, certainly, and some, by an act of possibly unconscious will, deny wonder altogether. Nevertheless, we all have an innate disposition to marvel at experiences and, for me, it's but a small step to call that element 'religious'. Everyone at some time has the need and the desire to make sense of existence. That making sense often takes forms that are not religious and so people embrace sport with passion, if they can afford it they possess things that indicate social status or they lay their ambitions on their children. All of us need to discover something that will bind life together for us. The Australian Broadcasting Corporation has a daily radio program in which invited guests are interviewed and asked to choose their favourite music to be played during the interview. The 'I'm not religious but ...' public figures almost invariably choose music with an unashamed religious origin: they'll choose a Monteverdi motet or a hymn of Hildegard of Bingen. Their professed irreligion makes no sense to me. For whatever reason – social pressure, perhaps – they seem embarrassed to admit to religion or God. Or perhaps they don't even know what it is they're denying.

Gerald Moore, the renowned accompanist, once told a story about two double-bass players who worked in the orchestra of an opera house. During the performance of a particular opera, there they were, the two of them, sawing away, back and forth, oomp, oomp, oomp pah, oomp, oomp, oomp. They had no idea what was going on up on the stage: all they could hear in their corner of the pit was their own oomp, oomp, oomp. One of the players told his colleague that he was taking the next night off and he thought he might go to hear the opera. 'What would you want to that for?' the other asked. 'I just thought I'd like to go, that's all,' was the reply. When, two nights later, the first double-bass player returned to the pit and took his place, he said excitedly to his neighbour, 'You've got no idea what's going on up there. It's wonderful. While we're thumping away here, there's a chorus singing the song of the toreador. It's wonderful, wonderful. I wish you could hear it.' Many people scrape and saw away, making a kind of music, and never realise the Something Else, whether it's Bizet's *Carmen* or Bach's *B Minor Mass*. They seem not to be open to the transcendent, the Other, the Beyond Self.

I suppose I could have oomp oomped my way through life and never known what was really going on in the opera house, but, for reasons to be explored later in this book, I have heard the chorus singing with gusto.

The consumerism philosophy has developed in Australia in a period of rapid economic growth in an increasingly secularised society. It's not too fanciful to trace this world view to American psychologists like Fromm, Maslow, and Rogers. Their emphasis was on the importance of personhood, on self-realisation ('self-actualisation', Maslow called it), on needs for belonging, for love and for status. The movement made its greatest appeal to a comfortable middle-class. Self-esteem was of major importance: to feel good about yourself was crucial. People who took on this view of the world of humankind believed they could do it themselves, realise themselves. They even intoned 'God helps those who help themselves' (which, it must be observed in passing, is very *un*biblical). From this world-view came encounter groups and self-help books. There was a kind of pietism in it all: it was intense and emotional. Its main thrust was not on new ways to believe or think but on new ways to experience. It was no longer a matter of 'I know' or 'I think' but rather 'I feel' and 'I guess'. No one was really to blame for anything because it was always someone else who was blameworthy.

Almost inevitably this cult of the 'Me' led to a moral relativism. If I *feel* something's Okay, then it is Okay. If I want something, then I should have it and now, whether it be an expensive wrist watch or a casual sexual experience. Nor is selfism simply a generational thing, a characteristic only of Baby Boomers and their younger siblings. Selfism reaches forward even into old age.

A pendulum-swing seems to have operated here. My parents' generation and even mine was out there serving, being neighbourly, getting involved in 'good works', even to the detriment of family life and relationships. Selflessness meant that there was no time to nurture the self. Then a realisation that life was passing by resulted in a new message, underlined by the media: what about yourself? Don't you owe yourself something? Not recognising our own needs was replaced by disregarding the needs of others. We became self-absorbed.

I have a handful of friends who have never really divested themselves of the kind of fundamentalist–evangelical experiences I once knew. In their sixties they have discovered spirituality. They have told me about their discovery. They have invited me to their meditation sessions. I've sat with them in a darkened room, with candles flickering, and listened to readings from the Middle Ages to the modern era. The aromatic candles, the long silences, the holding of hands gave a sense of nearness and calm. Nevertheless, it was all a 'feel-good' experience and – or so it seemed to me – focused on the self. To charge these friends of mine with existential narcissism is far too harsh, for they are honest and gentle people and dear to me. Yet to escape from a conservative

Christian ghetto community into this variant of New Age spirituality is no lasting guarantee of personal freedom.

When I was growing through my teens into my early twenties, I would see middle-aged and older couples walking together. Just that. Walking together. Perhaps in a formal way the wife's hand would be tucked into the crook of her husband's elbow, but often there was no physical linkage. Now it's different. I see retired couples walking together *holding hands*, almost desperately joined in defiance at the world. 'Look', my wife says, 'Clinging to the wreckage'. The image is apt. All they seem to have is each other, Their families and friends are out of touch or gone. So much has happened, so many changes in personal relationships, community and shared meaning. And the wreckage that's washed up isn't only that of lives but also of dreams, foundered on others' selfishness.

In the early Middle Ages the self was the immortal soul, the focus of personhood under God. But now we've created what a psychologist has called 'the empty self'. Its emptiness has constantly to be filled up with consumer products and with the search for self-realisation. The medieval self was strengthened and made whole by ritual, rituals at birth, marriage and death, at the turn of the seasons, at religious observances. We've lost many of our rituals. To take one: when I became a university academic in the early 1960s, it was the practice to lecture dressed in an academic gown. Within a decade this was dismissed as a quaint anachronism and the sense of occasion was, at least in the minds of some of us, diminished. It's interesting to see the return in schools of debutante balls and 'formals', with frothy confections of gowns and black ties and tails, an attempt to reinstate ritual. And more and more young Australians travel annually to Gallipoli to remember in dignified silence the Anzacs' courage: they sense a need to be there to practise remembering as an occasion. Most of our celebratory activities are pseudo-rituals, football Grand Finals and motor-racing Grands Prix. We need rituals, all of us, to mark experiences of significance, and religious observance is (or must I say, 'used to be'?) a source of ritual.

Someone once said that religion is never defeated, only degraded. We've seen through the second half of the twentieth century not the defeat but the successive degradation of religion. It's either been cheapened out of meaning or tightened into a rigid fundamentalism. What I'm doing in these memoirs is, in a sense, talking to myself, musing on what's happened. I want to embrace my religious experience and not merely accept it.

I think often about the will of God, particularly what I've already suggested we call his ultimate will. This ultimate will is to ensure that men and women recover a unity with the source of all being. Unless we're exceptionally fortunate, we pass through life stumbling from one grief or pain to another, one disappointment to another. George Steiner put it tellingly: 'The immense majority of human biographies are a grey transit between domestic spasm and oblivion'. I wouldn't want to put it as bleakly as that. There is much that is amazing, joyous and beautiful in human life, irrespective of social or intellectual status: some people out of horrors unimaginable can salvage a sense of delight in the world.

No one knew this human life better than Martin Luther and in his writings the word *trotz*, meaning 'in spite of' or 'nevertheless', echoes like the tolling of a great bell. He understood at depth the currents of intrigue and danger but kept on saying *trotz*, nevertheless. My enemies are ranged against me, nevertheless ... I've had to seek asylum in this desolate place, nevertheless ... I suffer the agonies of a physical disability, nevertheless . . . Neverthless, God is with me; nevertheless, God is my helper; nevertheless, God is my refuge. Nevertheless, the ultimate will of God will prevail. I love that word *trotz*. It's my faith.

That greatest of all Lutheran artists, J.S. Bach, had a wonderful constellation of certainties. One of the six parts of his Christmas Oratorio, the cantata for the First Sunday in the New Year, begins with an almost breathlessly joyous chorus.

Let Thy glory be hymned, O God!
Let praise and thanksgiving be prepared for Thee.
All the world extols Thee . . .

As the choir sings with an excited freshness, the woodwinds in the orchestra are chuckling away in a kind of holy glee. It's rapturous.

All our desire is fulfilled
Because Thy blessing fills us so gloriously with joy.

The cheerfulness and sunshine of the music is utterly transcendent. Of all my experiences of art, music and literature, this comes the nearest to expressing what I feel and know about what I believe.

I'm not so foolish as to think that the so-called high culture I've been admitted to (Raphael, Vivaldi, Buxtehude, Milton, Stanley Spencer) gives me some advantage in my search for a sustaining religious belief. We're not all born culturally equal. It's easier for some to bolster their faith with the testimony of great artists than for others. It seems unfair. Some believers have to do with less. But true faith is not elitist. This is simply the story of *my* transit which I don't believe is, under God, grey.

8. Aborigines, Expatriates, and a Death

I'd heard from Dad about a Baptist missionary working on the Yuendumu Native Settlement in the desert some 280 kilometres out of Alice Springs. Dad thought he was good value. Why didn't I write to him to see if he'd have me as a visitor? For despite my feeling quite settled at Adelaide High, the earlier dream of working with Aborigines had never quite left me. The missionary said he'd be delighted for me to come. I got a Native Affairs Branch permit and prepared to leave for the mission station in December 1952.

I'm sitting on my sleeping bag under a *witjuti* shrub, eating cold baked beans from a tin. Aboriginal men drift past in twos and threes. One of them stops and looks down at me.

'*Njundu bala njinyanji?*' He grins.

'*Bala*,' I grin back.

What am I doing here? How did I get here?

I finish my marks and end-of-year reports and Alf lets me off school a week early. I catch the Ghan on a Thursday at lunch time. All the railways people tell me is that we'll reach Alice Springs some time on Saturday. I'm trying to get to Yuendumu but through a curious set of circumstances I get a ride with old Pastor F.W. Albrecht when I arrive in Alice Springs. He's just back from Germany and wants to visit his Lutheran missionary settlements. We go to Jay Creek, Hermannsburg and Haast's Bluff. At Haast's Bluff I get invited to walk to Yuendumu with a visiting corroboree party, with a Ngalia man and some Arrarnta and Pitjantjatjara people, but the Patrol Officer, Les Wilson, won't let me. Says he can't be responsible. I have to go all the way back into Alice Springs, and wait until I can hitch a ride north-west to Yuendumu.

When I get there, I'm told there's going to be a big, big corroboree, an initiation ceremony for two local boys. People are still arriving. Nosepeg, the corroboree boss, whose head will some years later appear on an Australian postage stamp, and who I had previously met at Haast's Bluff, sees me in the settlement compound and asks me to come to the corroboree. I sense he just *likes* me. The tribesmen are meeting about twenty-five minutes walk from the settlement. I take my rucksack and some food and go. I have a pad and pencil and I decide to take notes. There are 114 men assembling in the scrub, as far as I can make out.

I watch the men adorning themselves in black, white and red ochre, puncturing their old sub-incision wounds with sharp mulga twigs and squeezing the blood from their penises down the inside of their legs. I watch their snake and their kangaroo and euro dances, listen to their chanting. I see reverence done to *tjuringa* and *wanigi*. I see the two novices being painted on chest and back with great deliberation. It all started on Saturday, this corroboree, and now it's Tuesday night and I can hardly keep awake, but I don't want to miss anything. It's the climax, now, the young boys laid on a 'table' made up of the backs of kneeling sponsors. In the fierce red-orange glare of the circumcision fire, their foreskins are cut, there's the sound of bull-roarers, the boys are hoisted onto the shoulders of their sponsors and are quickly borne off into the blackness of the scrub.

I lurched bone-weary back to the settlement. It was in darkness. I let myself in to the room I'd been given, collapsed onto the bed, pulled my boots off and fell into instant, deep sleep. Next thing, standing by the bed, is Pat Fleming, the Baptist missionary's wife. 'Dear boy,' she said cheerfully, 'You look buggered. Been asleep for twelve hours. Tea?'

Reverend Tom Fleming had been a POW in Changi and the malnutrition and beatings he'd suffered had left him with seriously impaired hearing. A suburban congregation was beyond him and he'd taken on the Yuendumu Baptist Mission from a hungry-for-souls evangelical. That was not Tom's way. He never made any attempt to deny belief or practice to the Ngalia (or, less politely the Warlpiri, 'those bastards from the west'). He ran church services on Sundays and when people came out of curiosity – three or four, a dozen – he told them the story of Jesus, Pat taught them some hymns and that was that. What Tom did do for years was to arbitrate in family and private disputes, see that children attended school, encourage the young men to learn a trade, and visit the Aboriginal camp to check on who was sick and needed treatment.

Early afternoon on the day after the corroboree, Tom told me he was going looking for the young initiates: did I want to come? I knew enough anthropology to realise that the boys had been secreted away by their 'uncles', their initiation sponsors, and were being given time to recover from the psychic shock of all that's happened to them. No one knew where they were. Of course. Tom stood in the dust with skinny camp dogs sniffing at his heels, and quietly said he wanted to see them and someone had pretty soon take him to where they were. Force of personality can be physical: Tom stared at the men until one of them pointed with his chin: 'Dat way.' Not good enough for Tom. 'Who's showing me?' They knew better than to try and stand up to the force of character and goodness in the man they called Tom-Father.

And one of them shamefacedly led us off through the *witjuti* bushes. We eventually found the boys sitting cross-legged under a bush shelter, their eyes glazed. From his haversack Tom produced a tin of penicillin powder and dusted the boys' weeping penises, touched each of the boys' heads, smiled at them and left the secret place.

That was my experience of Aboriginal people in the early 1950s. I found them wonderfully friendly, loving to stroke me, my arms, my cheeks, with their long, cold fingers. They were full of fun, laughed a lot in high pitched voices, took me into their lives, even though for only a few weeks, Japaljarri, Jupurrurla, Jungarrayi families, old Darby Jampijinpa. And that was my first and personal experience of missionaries. Not conservatives with only one path to God, but carers first. Someone should write an account of Tom Fleming's Yuendumu. I believe it was Tom's influence, saintly and flawed, that established Yuendumu as a cohesive community, that gave the Warlpiri a sense of their own worth, that led to the painting of the people's Dreamings, and the women's night patrol against drinking and the Australian Rules Football festival that takes in Western Australia, South Australia and the Territory.

Some twenty years later my two sons, Peter in 1970 and Peter and David in 1973, visited Yuendumu. Tom-Father and his wife were still there. Peter and David were given honorary skin-names by the Warlpiri elders, the clans of Jupurrurla and Japaljarri respectively, appropriate for my sons. For the Yuendumu people had remembered me after all that time. I have an ambivalent attitude to Australian Aborigines. I have eaten with desert people, been taken into their confidence, seen their happiness, giggled with them. I know my experience is limited to full-blood desert people who still went on walkabout, but at least it's something more than do-good bleeding hearts in middle-class suburbs have. Aborigines are not frail, whingeing, no-hopers in essence. They've been battered by drink and disease, but the best of them, that is, their essences, are noble, proud and courteous. I'm uneasy, even as a churchman, with city and town-based Aboriginal activists speaking for all Aborigines, as though Indigenous people in the back lanes of Redfern and St Kilda can somehow be equated with the Warlpiri and their kind. Tom Fleming told me once of the visit of a well-known Aboriginal activist to the Yuendumu settlement. The activist painted an alarming picture of the degradation and hopelessness of their brothers and sisters. When Darby Jampijimpa said that things were all right with them, the visitor snapped, 'What would an ignorant old blackfella like you know about it?'

I'm righteously angry about mining companies and their cavalier disregard for Aboriginal sacred places but I'm also aware of the complexities of Native Title issues. I know about massacres and abuses, about the so-called stolen generation, but I also recognise the social contexts in which these things occurred. I'm ashamed at the way Europeans have treated the Aboriginal people but merely throwing money at problems is not a guarantee of ameliorating them. There is no parallel between Afro-Americans and our indigenous people: the parallel is between native Amerindians and Aborigines. But even there the linkages are problematical: we have no equivalent to the North American Indian nations – no Mohawk nation, for example, which both hunted and planted. For me, it's all too hard. My belief-system wants me to show compassion and understanding, to try to get my consciousness around the idea of the spirit of land and the Dreaming. Until I can do that, I can't simply impose European sentimentality upon these dislocated and complicated problems.

One thing I do find wondrous and ineffable is the Indigenous people's sense of what we'd call the holy. Many years after my corroboree experience I stood at the Mutitjulu waterhole on that western side of Uluru and felt a palpable sense of spirit. This was a place that had a presence. There was something both immanent and transcendent. Maybe it was because generations back to the dawn of prehistory had come to this place and invested it with thoughtfulness and reflection and awe. I couldn't but remember that in 1605 the Portuguese Pedro Fernandez de Quiros made a landfall and in triumph called the place *Austrialia del Espiritu Santo*, the South Land of the Holy Spirit. There is something about the Australian landscape, plains and deserts, escarpments and rolling hills, waterfalls and seascapes, that, for those who need it, is spiritual, appealing to the human soul and its awareness of the Other.

When Tom Fleming died, the community put together themselves a memorial service and, movingly, under Tom's name on the cover they put 'He growed us up'. I don't care at all for the cheap shots made at missionaries. There are missionaries and missionaries. If my late adolescent dream of serving the Aborigines had come off, I hope I would have done what Tom did. Cared. Not made converts to Christianity, not counted heads in some sanctified census, but loved them as made in the image of God. It's still a popular sport to poke fun at or be vehement and even spiteful about missionary activity as though *every* missionary is in the mould of the nineteenth-century imperialists who saw the 'heathen' as living in the darkness of sin. With those missionaries I have very little patience: the best of missionaries put on penicillin powder and then pray.

I had by now fallen in love with Dorothy. I remember taking her in my arms on a New Year's Eve near the junction of Burke Road and High Street in East Kew, and, simply, falling in love with her at that moment. It was the year before I went to Yuendumu. We courted each other across the miles between Melbourne and Adelaide by exchanging gifts of books by C.S. Lewis and the then vastly popular dramatist, Christopher Fry, or so inscriptions in books still on our shelves suggest. It was difficult for Dorothy: however much her parents approved of me in principle, they were unhappy at the prospect of our marrying and going to live 'all that way away' in Adelaide.

It's hard to imagine now how far Adelaide was from Melbourne then. Today it's only an hour by air. Then, to travel it by road was a major journey, with risks of punctures and over-heating engines. Then, you went by train, overnight in the *Overland*, about fourteen hours. To fly was expensive. Even to ring up on the telephone was unusual. You couldn't dial direct, and you'd get 'Three minutes, caller, are you extending?' and wonder whether the operator had been listening to your conversation.

If Ian loved you, said Dorothy's parents, he'd come to Melbourne. So it wasn't easy for me, either. At one point I was so convinced it was all over that I burned all her letters. Then on the evening of 1 June 1953, Dorothy rang and said she'd come, would go anywhere with me. It was the very day that news had come through that Hillary and Tensing had conquered Everest.

In eighteen months we were married – by Dorothy's minister and my father – in the little Baptist church in North Balwyn and went to live in the manse with my father. We would pay no rent, but in lieu Dorothy would keep house. I'd been clattering around the suburbs on a 4¼ horse power Ariel motorbike and sidecar. Dorothy never quite got used to it but soon learned which way to lean on corners. We were young and, I see now, self-ish. Dorothy looked after Dad but never quite understood how conservative he was. Roast lamb, potatoes and peas was his idea of a meal, not more exotic dishes from the cookery classes Dorothy was taking or new recipe books. There was always that third party in the house. We felt cramped. It never occurred to us that Dad had his difficulties, too.

We had both gone to our marriage bed as virgins. How I know we loved each other is the way we adjusted ourselves to physical intimacy, how with tenderness we experimented in our search for what we came to call our sacrament. We never took love-making lightly. Nor was it over-earnest. We simply gave each other to each other. Years later, in a poem called 'Whose Is This Moment?', I wrote

Whose is this moment, when the house is empty of movement
save ours?
Above the bed hang
slow words of people and places, the past,
now and tomorrow. Your thigh warms between
my legs; my fingers trace your lips and nose.
Periphery becomes centre, words sounds,
and the fuse of flesh ignites, glows along
the length of life to spark and startle like lightning
all around in a sweet smell of peace.

It was like that, then, and is now, always, surprising us, refreshing us.

Whose is this moment, when the morning seeps across
the open window?
You will not wake, but lie
melted to my side, the soft fire flickering

still in your belly and breasts. Your eyes are dark
beneath their lids, dream-dark and safely
lost. I inch myself from the bed-clothes and see
you clutch the pillow. Your mouth is beautiful. You stir
again and burrow into my warmth that's left.

I was a member of the Modern Pickwick Club, a long-established Adelaide literary cultural group of, in the main, businessmen and academics. One of the club members I became friendly with was Peter Nossal, brother of Gus, of later national renown. Peter was in the university's Biochemistry Department and a resident tutor at the Roman Catholic Aquinas College. I remember going to Aquinas once to a ball. Dorothy found it impossible to get into the sidecar in her ballerina-length frock and had to ride behind me on the pillion seat, her skirt pulled up over her knees. Through Peter I had got to know the Rector of Aquinas, Father Michael Scott, SJ. Father Scott struck me as strong and dour, but he had a great social charm. He'd just produced a booklet on Christian belief, and one of his anecdotes made a lasting impression on me: it was just what I was looking for. He described being in a gallery, on the wall of which hung a gorgeous tapestry. There being nobody about, he lifted up a corner of the tapestry and looked at the underside. It was a tangle of straggly loose ends. But when he let the corner fall, there was the flower-pattern, gold, green, scarlet, blue, pink, in the most beautiful arrangement, orderly, harmonious. I knew that life could be a tangled mess, I knew that Dad knew that life could be a mess: what I needed to know was that there was sense somewhere. Could I believe that?

This was my first ever contact with a Catholic priest – almost my first contact with a Catholic anybody. For then, even in the 1950s, there was a great divide between Catholics and Protestants. Children called each other names across the divide, Protestant public servants complained about the way the Catholics looked after their own. I heard many stories of Methodists, Baptists, being passed over in promotion rounds by Catholics who had a co-religionist as departmental head. I began talking to friends about this Father Scott and his terrific booklet. Nobody showed any interest. They would never have said so, but they thought I was letting the side down, consorting with the enemy. Dad, however, seemed to think it was all right. It didn't bother him a bit; he thought the booklet was 'useful and helpful, son'.

Brian Elliott, my thesis supervisor in the university's English Department, had just returned from sabbatical leave. One night he invited Dorothy and me to a slide night at his home. Innocent romantics as we were, we gasped and sighed as landscapes and street scenes clicked onto the screen. Brian told us we should go overseas while we were still young and we were all too ready to listen. Without telling Dad – perhaps we were cruel to do it but he had already put us off going overseas after we were married – we booked our passages on P&O's *Arcadia*. And then Dorothy became pregnant. We believed there was no turning back: we were prepared to cut all ties. Dad said nothing.

Our baby was born in Adelaide's principal maternity hospital, late on a hot February night, and unlike today when most fathers choose to be present at the birth, I wasn't allowed to see the child because visiting hours did not allow it. The following day I was busy teaching, or going through the motions, in a kind of automatic response: I wanted to see Dorothy and my heir. After school I hurtled to North Adelaide on the motor-bike and found a very sore and sorry-for-herself mother. The baby had torn his way into the world and his mother was sitting on a mass of stitches, while he yelled in the nursery.

I felt so sorry for Dorothy. Concerned but elated I went home, to find Dad at the back door, pipe in hand and a twisted smile on his face. 'I saw your son before you did: I went in this morning as a clergyman and they let me have time with them.' What could I say? Couldn't I have my baby to myself? Were Dad's needs so desperate? They were, I was to realise much later.

Baptists don't christen or baptise babies: that's left for consenting and confessing adults. Our sacrament we call 'dedication'. The minister asks the parents and the congregation to promise to bring the child up into a knowledge of Jesus Christ, and not to allow any impediment to growth into a Christian faith. Dad dedicated our first born Peter: held him in the church before us and in the name of the Father, Son and Holy Ghost, offered him into the Lord's keeping. It was a tender moment for me. And Dad had in his arms a future he perhaps had not dared hope for. His smile took on a rare softness.

We had to embark in Melbourne because *Arcadia* wasn't calling in to Adelaide. A week before we left Dorothy went to Melbourne with Peter to be with her parents, and I spent those days in an uneasy truce with my father. When I left for Melbourne by train, I stood awkwardly on the carriage steps, looking down at Dad. We shook hands and he said to me, 'I don't suppose I'll be here when you get back.'

'Don't be silly, Dad,' I retorted, stunned. 'We're only going for three years teaching and my masters course. That's no time at all. Of course you'll be here.'

'Bye, son,' he said, and the train began to slide along the platform.

There was no way I could have got a teaching job from

Australia. I'd have to wait until we got to England and see what was on offer. I suppose it was a gamble. Young couple with three-month-old baby, travelling on G-deck with no air-conditioning, utterly innocent, when we stopped at Bombay, of smelly and abject poverty. After nearly four weeks we saw the southern coast of England through a dank, grey mist of an English summer morning, then were bullied for no good reason by immigration officers.

Through a business associate of my father-in-law's I got a job as a filing clerk in a firm of Lloyd's brokers in the City of London. I earned ten pounds a week, while our bed, breakfast and dinner rental at Oak House in Putney came to ten guineas, and already we began nibbling at our capital.

Those three months in London weren't a good time for Dorothy. Peter was a demanding baby and Dorothy was feeding him herself: the hungrier Peter got, the hungrier Dorothy got. Oak House was full of old ladies who didn't care for the sound of a baby crying, and she spent weekdays walking Peter through the streets of Putney or up to the Common in our low-slung foreign-looking pram, and made conversation with anyone who would talk to her. For me, it was all right. I had something to sustain me.

When my father's church at St Peter's was installing a pipe-organ, I had a vacation job as general dogsbody to the builder. I crawled under the church floor with lead tubing, lined up pipes in numbered order, boiled up pots of glue. I felt I owned that organ. And it was played by one of the Sunday School boys, David Merchant, already an organist of great promise. Later, one of my closest colleagues at Adelaide Boys' High School was the Director of Music, Alan Tregaskis, who was, in my view, one of the country's finest organists: I've never heard anyone play the Mozart organ works better.

I became a great listener to organ music. Now, in London, my listening was enriched.

It's just after half past twelve. I've done a late morning round of the brokers' desks, picked up files no longer required, returned them to the banks of grey metal cabinets and now sit quietly in a corner eating my sandwiches. In ten minutes I shall go to the washroom and then take another ten minutes brushing my jacket, combing my hair, scrubbing my nails, anything, until 12.57. There are other clerks of course, in white starched collars and navy suits, and at 12.57 we move, and the common calculation is sharply accurate: at 1.00 we all step together into Leadenhall Street. I turn left and run. Today I have little time. Left again into Lime Street across Fenchurch Street between lumbering buses. Phillpot Lane, weaving the pavements to the gutters, taxis and lorries in Eastcheap, and I glance up at the Great Fire of London Monument as I, sentimentalist, do every day, twice a day, even, and the ball of brass flames flashes in the watery sun. In Lower Thames Street the stink of Billingsgate fish, and I'm through the iron gateway into the shadowed and dark churchyard of St Magnus the Martyr. I pause by the church door to regain my breath. I look at my watch. Four minutes past one. I enter the church and a glum verger passes me a duplicated program. I know this church. I know where to sit. I see I am the only one. I am the audience.

I do this three times and sometimes four times a week. I bolt from my firm to lunch-hour organ recitals at St Mary Woolnoth, St Stephen Walbrook, St Edmund, King and Martyr, St Michael Cornhill, St Peter Cornhill, St Helen, Bishopsgate. I know the musty wood smell of these churches, the deep patina of pew-ends, the cold flagstoned floors. Today it is St Magnus. I love this Alexander Jordan organ, set in its hardwood case in the gallery above the porch. It has its own voice, unlike, say, St Botolph's or St Ethelburga's. I love this church, remembered by T.S. Eliot in *The Waste Land*.

But it's not only the interior Ionian white and gold splendour. As I sit waiting for the organist (he's a little late – is he hoping for an audience of perhaps two?), I marvel at this church of Christopher Wren's from the late seventeenth century that is rooted so firmly at the foot of London Bridge. The sky outside choked by the ugly bulk of Adelaide House, and I marvel at the delicate complexity of the spire that wrestles free from the crush of eight-storey blocks.

A door bangs. I turn and see the young organist slide along the bench and clunk his stops. He's wearing a Fair Isle jumper. It's a mixed bag, this program, opening with a wistful Soler reflection and then (I hear it often at these recitals) the Liszt fugal exploration on the letters BACH. Two meditations follow, one on the nativity by Flor Peeters and one by Karg-Elert, long, grim, jagged, dark, on the Crucifixion. There's a pause. The young man flexes his shoulders, I see, and then with the courage of one who has seen beyond the printed page, sweeps into J.S. Bach's Dorian mode *Toccata and Fugue*.

I wait through the first bars for the thunder of the footpedals. If ever Albert Schweitzer was right, it was about the galloping horses motif in Bach's music. I look unseeing down the church, past the elegant white columns and their gold-leafed capitals, to the reredos, which shimmers and moves out of focus. I can only hear, hear the insistent drumming of hooves, the certain cavalry advance. It's not a gallop, this performance, but a controlled canter, brisk and high-stepping. The concluding bars reign in the horses, the hooves stamp into sudden silence. I can't swallow. There are tears in my eyes. I clap, looking over my shoulder. The young man (my age?) waves at me and smiles.

I put two shillings in the box as I leave and I cannot hear the rattling gabble outside. A Billingsgate fishmarket porter with an empty trolley hurries near and shouts 'Oi!' from under his smelly leather hat. My head rings with Johann Sebastian's sixteen notes all the way back to Leadenhall Street. As I slip into the filing department, my Canadian boss looks up from his desk. And smiles. I smile back.

These recitals opened a new world of worship for me. All my experiences had been in non-Conformist churches: plain, relatively unadorned, the church more auditorium than sanctuary. We Baptists, Methodists and all the rest, put most store by the preaching of the Word, with the pulpit as focus. If we were to 'see Jesus', as John's gospel had it, then it was to be through the arguments and persuasion of the minister in his sermon. We had no need, we thought, for the 'inexplicable splendour of Ionian white and gold'. Certainly no need for candles: *that* was Popery. Yet in some strange way I came to feel comfortable in those ancient places of worship decorated with carved angels and smelling stalely and sweetly of incense.

Dorothy and I were silly and romantic in our moments together while in London. We did the Tower of London and Hampton Court and all that (even with Peter), ooh'ing and ah'ing like the good deferential colonials we were. Then I got a job teaching English and a little Latin in a somnolent market town called Crediton. It was in Devon, a short bus ride from Exeter. Back in Exeter after the interview, at which I'd been given the post on the spot, I had time to spare and went into the cathedral, not to thank God for answered prayer (I was past that) but to express gratitude and to acknowledge my delight to him (I'd given away the capital H). I sat in the nave of this tall, grand building, listening to the echoes of footsteps. I looked up at the glorious vault, for all the world like a stately avenue of trees, linking branches overhead. For six hundred years people had been coming into this numinous place to sit and wonder and feel. That five minutes or so remains with me still.

If I'd been silly and romantic with Dorothy in London, now I was even sillier. The school I was to teach at was a minster's choir school founded in 739 AD, three hundred years *before* the Norman Conquest. I couldn't believe it. No wonder we colonials showed all that deference. If you really wanted to, you could even trace the school's prehistory back to St Boniface, the great Christian missionary to Germany in the early 700s. St Boniface was born in Crediton. I was enraptured by my newly acquired sense of the on-going history of Christian belief.

Dorothy and I looked after a senior boarding house in a rambling Victorian building at the back of the school property. One night in my second term there I was called to Main School to the telephone. It was my father's brother. Dad was in hospital and not expected to come out of his coma. My uncle said there was no point in my trying to come home: I'd be too late. I reeled out into the cold March night. I didn't know what to feel. Grief? Anger? A sense of freedom? Why hadn't my father told me how ill he was? There had been no suggestion, no hint, that he was unwell. He'd said nothing in those days we had alone before I left Adelaide. The news was like a right hook to my heart.

Years later I heard from my father's church secretary how Dad died. It was a cancer that he had been harbouring for some time – surely he knew when he said goodbye to me? – and it had flared up and engulfed him.

Reg Althorp, the church secretary, had contacted Dad's brother in Melbourne. Hector had remained within the Brethren fold, had done well in business and was a leading figure in Brethren circles. He sat by Dad's hospital bed and took from his pocket one of those little New Testaments that have the Psalms appended. He began to read

Yea, though I walk through the valley
of the shadow of death, I will fear no
evil: for thou art with me,
Thy rod and thy staff they comfort me . . .

Dad, with some effort, brought his hand up from beneath the bedclothes, avoided the tubes up his nose and pushed away his brother's hand, and the little Testament. 'Put it away, Hector,' he said. 'Put it away. I know all about that.' They were the last words he spoke.

9. Career

I didn't know how to handle my father's death. Spring was coming early to the West Country that year and for weeks I was afflicted for the first time in my life with hay fever, suffering so severely that often I couldn't get my breath. I had all the symptoms of asthma.

It was guilt. We were overseas against Dad's wishes. I hadn't been with him when he was dying. I'd never told him how much I admired his courage. I'd been a delinquent son.

On the other hand, my father had never praised me. I won the university's poetry prize and he said, 'Good, son.' When I graduated, all he said was 'Good, son.' My self-esteem in his presence was always low. That's why I was a show-off, a public buffoon. I craved applause. I got plenty, but that was different; it wasn't Dad. I was a deacon in his own church, I sang in his choir, I taught in his Sunday School. In the wider Baptist denomination I was on youth committees, always regarded as 'Norman's son'. What did he want before he could tell me I was doing all right?

Anger throbbed in me. One of the great regrets I have is the way the sanctimonious Brethren in his family crippled my father emotionally. Perhaps he was inclined to be inward anyway, but I believe his fundamentalist upbringing choked him. At times during his second marriage I saw or thought I saw him become freer with his feelings, but there was on the whole little evidence.

As I was his only child, I, too, learned to be inward about deep things. Perhaps we were just bad for each other. Now, I thought, I was free at last.

I had enrolled as a Master's candidate in Education in the University of Southampton. The Professor of Education was Adelaide-born F.W. (Freddie) Wagner, who had planted a gum tree in front of his department's building. My thesis supervisor was Dr K.M. Lobb, a warm-hearted Methodist churchman. Dr Lobb (I never thought of calling him Ken) once invited me to a seminar conducted by the Cambridge don, T.R. (Tommy) Henn. Not because I wanted to attend (I'd never heard of Henn) but out of respect to Dr Lobb, I went. It was an all-day affair. Henn led us through a discussion of *Antony and Cleopatra*, *King Lear*, *Troilus and Cressida*, and outlined for us the Elizabethan view of the world. As an aside at one point he referred to 'the trajectory of the King'. I can't speak for anyone else there, but I was bowled over, stunned, made giddy.

From examinations of belief-systems in a range of cultures, Henn told us, anthropologists had postulated a pattern in the lives of great men of myth. It went like this: a King, the son of a King, has a magical birth from an unusual conception, and soon after his birth an attempt is made on his life. He flees his homeland to live with foster-parents, returns at manhood, gains victory over a would-be usurper and marries a princess. He then loses favour with the populace. There is a revolt and, together with malefactors, he dies a mysterious death at the top of a hill, and his body is never buried.

I sat there staring at my notes. Somehow I roused myself to copy down a diagram to illustrate human physiology as interpreted in Shakespeare's day. But this 'trajectory of the King' spun round and round in my head. Another revelation. The Jesus story fits, I told myself. The virgin birth, the flight into Egypt, the re-appearance at manhood, the fall from favour, the death with brigands on the hill of Calvary, the body never buried in the earth. It was exciting and it comforted me. We're right after all, we Christians: we fit, we belong.

In the time we spent in England, nearly five years, this was only one of a number of formative religious experiences. During the middle and late 1950s the earnest, unsmiling Biblical scholar William Barclay was a talking head on television. He looked straight at the camera, at us, and talked. No gimmicks, no visuals, just old Willy talking about life in Palestine, or the links between the life of Jesus and the Old Testament, or the puzzle of the resurrection. The Sunday afternoon *Brain's Trust* program, talking heads again, always had radical clerics on its panel, like the Anglicans' Mervyn Stockwood or some chubby, bright-eyed Roman Catholic such as the Abbot of Downside. Dietrich Bonhoeffer's *Letters and Papers from Prison* was doing the rounds still: C.S. Lewis had put together three of his earlier books, revised and amplified, into one title, *Mere Christianity*. Before leaving home I'd come to know J.B. Phillips *Letters to Young Churches*. As I recall, he rendered a verse from 1 Corinthians 13 as 'Love does not compile statistics of evil' and I liked that – though in Phillips' final version it was gentler. Now this translator brought out a collection of little essays called *Your God is Too Small* (my copy, I see, is inscribed 'I.V. Hansen, June 1957'), in which he explored destructive images of God, like 'Resident Policeman', 'Pale Galilean' and 'God-in-a-Box'. The one that caught hold of me was 'Parental Hangover'. It went for me right back to the episode with my parents and chewing gum cards, and the message I got from Phillips was that I'd just have to grow out of it if I wanted my faith to 'blossom out into joy and confidence'. It was a helpful book.

There was a continual ferment in religious ideas. We got them from our regular preachers in our churches in London, Exeter and Portsmouth. The Baptist denomination in

Australia tended to take its strength from the working and lower middle classes, or at least from the accepting attitudes of those groups. The church people I knew in Adelaide were on the whole lazy thinkers when it came to matters of belief. Baptists in those days tended to be exclusive, suspicious of other denominations and particularly the Roman Catholics and the Church of *England* (as it was then – the cultural cringe: why the Church of England in *Australia*?)

But here we were, Dorothy and I, in England, and we found it was quite different. Some major policy makers in the World Council of Churches came from the British Baptists: that was a surprise to us. And the preaching we sat under each Sunday was always thought-provoking and intellectually challenging – was it only curious that two of our ministers were Welsh? And perhaps the style of preaching came from the fact that our congregations had a greater proportion of professionals than we were used to finding.

I don't want to think that England shaped me in a religious sense. I was patronised so often by teaching colleagues, even by too-clever-by-half senior boys. I'd put up with their snide remarks about convicts and cultural deserts ('Do you have symphony orchestras?') and often found the Poms insufferably condescending. Yet finally I have to admit that this time in England (I aged from 27 to 31) firmed my evolving faith. The C.S. Lewises, the Mervyn Stockwoods and the Willy Barclays gave me things to think hard about, while at a personal level, kindly and gentle souls understood me and were there to listen to me, like our minister, colleagues and neighbours.

We lived in the Old Dart for nearly five years. I was working the whole time, Dorothy was housekeeping and mothering; we were not tourists. There was a lot we didn't do, a lot we didn't see.

We went to Denmark, a romantic fancy of mine, thinking

I'd find long-lost relatives. According to family tradition a Danish forebear, a seaman, jumped ship in Gippsland, Victoria, in the 1830s. It was like finding a Smith in London. But we did manage while away to take an Easter journey from Oslo to Bergen with our ten-month-old son, who was already walking.

We stayed two weeks with a Catholic family in Vorarlberg, Austria. We toured Scotland for Dorothy's sake, because her mother was a Scot. I went on school trips to Wales, Germany and Belgium.

I twist the kaleidoscope: one of the boys in our Crediton boarding house, torn by pangs of unrequited passion for the headmaster's voluptuous daughter makes an attempt at suicide by slashing his wrists ('The feeblest cat-scratches you've ever seen,' says Dorothy when the bandages are removed), and throws the whole school into a frenzy of gossip. We're in a car accident in Oxford where I'm doing research and our wrecked vehicle is written off. I lose ten Duke of Edinburgh Award boys on the featureless rolling emptiness of Dartmoor overnight and for twenty-four hours. We're short of money and at first unbeknown to us Dr Lobb pays my Master's degree fees for the last two years.

There was no Earl's Court enclave for us, no Kangaroo Valley where we could feel at home with other expatriate Australians. We had come to live in England and with the English. It wasn't easy. We were patronised, taken advantage of and caricatured. A friend of ours on the staff of that Queen Elizabeth school in Devon reported to us an exchange in the Common Room: 'I really think it's disgraceful the way the Head has let the Hansens clean up and decorate those rooms in the San, instead of having it done for them.'

And then the riposte: 'It's no great matter. They're Orstralians, they're used to roughing it.'

There was nobody we knew who could possibly appreciate how difficult things were for us, not often but from time to time. In all three schools I was to teach at I was made form master of the most difficult and recalcitrant class; 'You'll manage them. You Orstralians are pretty tough.' It was in fact four years before we met another Australian.

In our time overseas we never had a visit from family. Phone calls were for us horrendously expensive and we never considered them. I reflect on young people today 'doing Europe' with instant phone contact, email, and a credit card for all their needs. Dorothy, a dutiful daughter, wrote a letter home every week, hundreds of them in total, but we only had each other, really, a situation stressful in itself. We'd either come through or it would all end.

From Crediton, which was only a one-year appointment, I got a senior English position (Post of Special Responsibility, it was called) in a local education authority grammar school for boys in Portsmouth. Through Baptist connections from our church in Exeter we were able to rent a rather miserable terrace house. We were fortunate, because finding affordable rent in a naval dockyard city where service personnel were given subsidised housing was difficult. We didn't know at first that we would be living on the wrong side of the tracks. In two years only one of my teaching colleagues ever visited; the others snobbishly found excuses not to accept our invitation. The friends we had were either near neighbours or church people.

One Sunday afternoon in spring we went in our elderly Morris exploring Hampshire villages. I remember stopping by a churchyard where large rhododendron bushes were flaming purple and there were spring birdsongs in the trees. It was a magical afternoon, full of presences. That evening, blissfully tired, Dorothy and I went upstairs as usual to bed but by two o'clock she was wide awake. The contractions were coming powerful and regular. 'I think we should go,' she whispered, so as not to disturb little Peter asleep in the next room. There was no one we knew intimately enough to call on (we didn't have a phone, anyway), so we tip-toed out of the house, leaving Peter. The car started first turn of the key and we drove the deserted Portsmouth streets to Southsea and the Eddystone Nursing Home where Dorothy's GP had booked her in: twice on the way there I stopped while Dorothy writhed on the back seat until she said, 'Okay, drive on.' We stood in the hallway of the nursing home and I watched while a marmalade cat brushed against Dorothy's legs. A sister, her hair in curlers, appeared and took charge and I drove back to Peter, mercifully still fast asleep.

Our second son came into the world slidingly and slippery without any assistance from anyone and with only brief discomfort to his mother who gave birth to him in the upstairs labour room while the night sister was with a labouring woman downstairs. He weighed eight pounds six ounces and had a great head of black hair. We called him David Norman, after my father, and he simply slept and fed, slept and fed.

Dorothy had earlier had a threatened miscarriage and was confined to bed for several weeks, lying there day after day while a kind friend cared for Peter while I went off to work. Now this new child was so placid and serene (after his rumbustious brother). We were so thankful to have him alive and in one piece but we wondered for some time whether he wasn't retarded as a result of the near miscarriage. We couldn't know and wouldn't have dared believe he'd win academic prizes and scholarships later in life.

My Southampton thesis dealt with the development of English in the secondary school curriculum and entailed an historical account of how the mother-tongue came to replace

Latin in old foundations like Queen Elizabeth's School in Crediton and better known schools like Eton and Harrow.

As a result of my investigations I'd developed an interest in private schools or, as the English perversely call them, public schools. I thought it'd be interesting to teach in one. I knew the Westminsters and the Rugbys wouldn't be interested in a colonial with no social connections but I did secure a job at a minor public school on the border of London and Kent, called Eltham College. We were given a flat in a large Victorian house that had once been the headmaster's residence and which we shared with the chaplain and his family and the music master and his wife. Through tall plane trees we had a view of the school chapel and one of the playing fields. There was snow in winter and crocuses in spring: it wasn't silly but it was certainly romantic.

I didn't know until we'd taken up residence that the school had been originally jointly founded in 1842 by the London Missionary Society and the Baptist Missionary Society. It was then called the School for the Sons of Missionaries; there was already a school for the daughters of missionaries, Walthamstow Hall, in Essex. From Blackheath the school moved in 1912 to the former Royal Naval School in Mottingham and was renamed Eltham College.

I was beside myself with pleasure. Not only was this a public school, albeit a lesser-known one, but it was a non-Conformist foundation. The two school chaplains were, in fact, Baptists of the liberal persuasion I felt so comfortable with. Dorothy and I were welcomed warmly into the small community that included 500 boys, 130 of them boarders. We had boarders over for tea, we watched important rugger matches. It *was* romantic.

Apart from providing a service to Baptist and Congregationalist missionaries, Eltham had two claims to fame. The first was that a member of the teaching staff in Blackheath days, a W.H. Balgarnie, was the original of James Hilton's fictional master in *Goodbye Mr Chips*. The second was that an Old Boy, Eric Liddle, set a world record for the 400 metres in the Paris Olympic Games of 1924 and then electrified the world of sport by refusing on religious grounds to run in the Games' 100 metres heats on a Sunday. The Liddle story was re-told in the film *Chariots of Fire* in 1981.

One aspect of Eltham life jarred on me. The missionary parents of boarders were often very demanding. Their sons won't have seen them for two or three years, they come home from furlough and are so busy with the Lord's work, travelling Britain on deputation, speaking and preaching, that they can barely find time to visit their boys. More than once it was said by these servants of the Lord, 'We're giving our lives to Jesus in jungles and mountains, so in return *you* can look after our sons.' There were two missionaries in particular I didn't like. They were so filled with evangelical importance it puffed them out like farmyard chooks. They were blunt and curt in their dealings with the boarding house staff, as though they could hardly spare any time for the school. It certainly wasn't, to use a phrase from my EU days, a good witness.

I had once with my father raised the matter of bearing witness to the faith after one of his deacons had behaved in a most un-Christ-like manner in a business dealing and my father said, 'Yes, but just imagine what he'd be like if he wasn't in the church.' Small comfort, I thought. But it had come back to me as I got angry with these self-important parents. They returned in memory to me forty years later as I read Barbara Kingsolver's novel *The Poisonwood Bible*, in which a Baptist missionary preacher is so consumed with his passion for the Word of God that he doesn't see or even care what's happening to his wife and children.

I've known some totally admirable missionaries, like Tom Fleming in Central Australia or Dane Mountford in Irian Jaya, but they were scarcely the stereotypical; they were eccentric in the sense of being off-centre. What appealed to me were stories I heard of Roman Catholic missionaries to China incorporating fireworks into the celebration of the Mass. That is the whole point, to make adjustments to the prevailing culture. What I had against some of the missionaries at Eltham was that they saw themselves in an unbroken succession from the 1850s and Victorians like David Livingstone. Livingstone was of his time. He treated his wife as a chattel, but so did most Victorians. He believed that God was an Englishman, but so did most Victorians. He called Africa the dark continent because he knew the darkness of sin blotted out the rays of God's glory, but so did most Victorians. He held passionately to the belief that the only way to save the heathen from the wrath of the Almighty was to dress them in European clothes and muster them in thatched churches, but so did most Victorians. Some of the Eltham College missionary parents were bombastic anachronisms who clung tenaciously to Victorian attitudes in matters of life and faith.

With regret, for we were happy at Eltham, we came home. Our Peter was ready to start school and if we didn't move then, we'd never return. We went to Melbourne to live, because Dorothy's family were there, and there was nobody for me in Adelaide. We'd been away nearly five years and spent money we could ill-afford keeping up a photographic slide record of people and places.

Few people were really interested in what we'd been doing. It was as though we were traitors. While we'd been away there had been a generation shift. Our age-peers were interested in houses, furnishings, cars, and not the things we were interested in. I don't say this with any trace of intellectual snobbery: it was just a fact. Our age-peers were all settled in careers and were earning good salaries; we had no money and few prospects. We'd become flexible, I suppose, having learned to change and adjust. Now we'd returned to a place that Robin Boyd saw as *The Australian Ugliness*, the Holdens with the two-tone colours and ample chrome, the brick veneers sprawling out into orchard-and farm-land. I remember how people I knew were outraged by Alan Seymour's play, *The One Day of the Year*, about the Anzac legend, and how I found I had no problem with it. And how I got excited by Peter Coleman's symposium, *Australian Civilization*, causing my age-peers to think I was an unrepentant Leftie.

With the small legacy my father had left me we bought a Holden station wagon, 'Australia's own car', and drove to Adelaide with the boys to see old friends. It turned out that Dad had left strict instructions in his will that all his sermons were to be destroyed. All those hundreds and hundreds of sermons, written out in full, gone. My disappointment was laced with left-over anger. How could he do this to me? He knew I'd have loved to have access to them. The will also stipulated that all his library was to go to the South Australian Baptist Theological College. I'd used his books often, he knew that, so why deny them to me? He must have had terrible moods of bitterness. But things weren't as bad for me as I thought. The Secretary of the Baptist Union and a friend of Dad's, Rev. Cliff Aldis, had put all Dad's books aside, and gave me first choice before handing the remainder over to the College. That way I came into possession of a number of ageless reference books like concordances and Biblical commentaries, a selection of things that he'd given me to read at some stage. Even more important to me was to find inside the back covers of two of the books two of Dad's handwritten sermons that had escaped destruction. I treasure them, though I'm sometimes not sure why.

After a term's temporary teaching at a Melbourne private school, I was appointed senior housemaster at the Presbyterian Haileybury College, then in South Road, Brighton. I thought this would be my life. Dorothy and I looked after seventy boarders and soon became part of the school community. I found my English teaching fulfilling and to our delight Dorothy became pregnant again.

My boarding house staff knew when the birth was due and it only needed a gentle knock on a door to say we were off to hospital and they would look after our two little chaps (see how you pick up language?). This time I would be present at the birth.

I'd been schooled by Jim Sinclair, Haileybury's wonderful doctor, and at about 10.30 pm I was at Dorothy's bedside, holding her hand, whispering encouragement, wiping her brow, doing all the attentive things expectant fathers do. And I did them until the nursing sister told me the imminent birth was a posterior presentation and would take some time. I was there with an exhausted Dorothy and I was angry at her pain and discomfort: she looked so pale and stressed. When the morning shift came on the new sister told me I was only in the way and it would be better if I went back to school. The baby would be some time coming. I felt cheated. Just before lunch Dorothy gave birth to Jane Alexandra, the news was phoned through to the boarding house and as if by magic a huge pink bow appeared at the top of the flagpole above the school flag.

The school had a religious life, minor, certainly, but genuine. I became involved in school assemblies and Sunday evening chapel services with the boarders. I worked in with the school chaplain. Yes, I thought, this suits me.

Then, late one afternoon towards the end of my second year I had a phone call from someone who called himself Dr Edgar French. He was, he said, from Melbourne University's Faculty of Education. He'd read a recently published article of mine in the *Australian Journal of Education* (it was, in fact, part of a chapter from my Southampton thesis) and he wondered whether I'd be interested in having a talk 'about things'. Would the following Thursday afternoon be all right?

What could this mean, I wondered. Perhaps they're going to let me extend my Southampton study into the Australian scene. So I went. On the appointed day I was ushered into the study of the then only professor W.H. Frederick. Also present was this Dr French, with Associate Professor W.V. Aughterson and Senior Lecturer Miss Wilma Hannah. I was suddenly very nervous. Professor Frederick was bouncy and cheerful. After introductions, Freddy, behind his neat desk, rubbed his hands together and said, 'Well now, Mr Hansen, how'd you like to come and work for us?'

I was flabbergasted. All I could think to say, weakly, was: 'What would I have to do?'

'Aha!' he said, 'What would you like to do?'

I mumbled that I was experienced in English teaching and before I knew it, I was being told that if I wanted to, I could start as a lecturer in the Diploma of Education program the very next year, only months away. I later discovered that Dr French had checked me out with the Haileybury school chaplain, whom he knew well.

I recount this in detail for two reasons. It shows how independent and free-thinking universities were in the early 1960s, especially in professional faculties. Secondly, it marked the beginning of a new stage in what could be called my religious journey. I would remain with the university's Faculty of Education for nearly thirty years.

We chose church schools for our children because at that time such schools never apologised for their witness to Christian faith and practice. We didn't quite believe that these schools could call out religious commitment in the previously uncommitted, but we did believe that they would affirm students who brought a faith stance from home. And they did, with regular religious observances in the school's life and with intelligent Religious Education programs. Which is more than I can say for such schools at the turn of the millennium, whether they be minor Catholic order schools or socially prestigious 'public schools'. They've sold out to the bottom line, to school as business, to a vague and undemanding ethical sense only; the transcendent is no longer of much account. In their place as religious foundations have sprung up fundamentalist schools often locking their students in a ghetto of belief: the pendulum, as pendulums will, has swung back too far. Meanwhile, the mainstream independent schools have allowed themselves to get caught up in a success ethic. They've become competitive and the victims of faddish expansionism, like building performing arts centres, grand front fences and Early Learning Centres. Business Managers and Development Officers mean a culture of selling a product. Schools become glittering and expensive and the gulf between the educational haves and have nots widens and widens. That's a social injustice that rankles with me when I think back to those times in the 1970s when I was, perhaps by default, an advocate for non-government schools. I believed then that they were serious about seeing the education of the whole person undergirt with a religious awareness. At the same time I wanted and still hope for government schools to offer the kind of committed teaching and planning I know they are capable of. But I digress, as they say.

Under arrangements prevailing at that time, the university provided our house loan. My father-in-law gave us a second mortgage and Dorothy took in two student boarders for two years. ('I've got *five* children,' she'd sometimes sigh) until a school poetry anthology I'd had published brought in wonderful royalties. In those days a single book could be set for public examination candidates and the author and publisher assured of thousands of sales every year. My royalties went to the mortgages and to school fees.

The climate within the Faculty of Education was congenial. It was jokingly said that appointments to the staff were alternately Catholic and Protestant, Catholic for Associate Professor Aughterson and Protestant for Professor Frederick, an enthusiastic Methodist. When I joined the full-time staff it numbered twenty or more and of those, at least fifteen had regular church affiliations, Catholics, Anglicans, Methodists, Presbyterians and me, the sole Baptist: we sat on church and denominational committees, were Sunday School teachers or lay-preachers and wrote for church journals and magazines. That is, we shared a common culture, and that made our functioning as a department comparatively relaxed. At one point, I recall, we had on our staff two Protestant clergymen and two Catholic priests. For many years there were three of us who were PKs. There was little awkwardness and little unreasonableness in our meetings. We got on.

As for the intellectual sense in the place, it was at least earnest. Most of us in those early days had come from secondary school classrooms, ex-teachers of some reputation. We'd not had much time for purely academic pursuits and now learned and specialised on the job. I can't remember a colleague I'd have called lazy, not in the early days. We enjoyed each other's company, both professionally and socially. I want to believe (and why shouldn't I?) that the *esprit* we knew had to do with the fact that we were a company of believers. We were none of us proselytisers or evangelicals but carried with us an unstated common world view. I'm sure in a subtle way this informed a lot of what went on in the university's Barry Building where we were housed.

After I'd been there some years, an articulate student who went on to have a long if somewhat eccentric career at one of Melbourne's well-known independent schools bailed me up after an evening's tutorial.

'Tell me, are you a Marxist or a Christian?' he demanded.

'Why do you ask?' I countered.

'Well, I've been observing you and the way you do what you do and I reckon that because of your commitment to your subject and your respect for the individual, you've got to be either a Marxist or a Christian. Which is it?'

'I'm a Christian,' I said.

'Fair enough,' he said, turned on his heel and was gone.

So I became an academic, whatever that word means. I suppose I thought it might mean that between lectures I could wander around the campus, sit under a tree and read. I was greatly mistaken. I was busier than I'd ever been in a school: preparing lectures, organising school practice placements for students and supervising their classroom performances, visiting schools, conducting in-service programs for teachers, it went on and on. But I was in my early thirties and full of energy. I managed.

That I was a university person worked two ways in my church circles. It had a severe negative effect. The working- and middle-class orientation of Baptists made them very suspicious of anything to do with universities. Universities were where young people lost their faith. Universities were places of free thinking and sin. University people were too clever, too ready to belittle religion, were immoral: you hear so many stories, don't you?

There was one thing going for me, Baptist tradition. For Baptists put great store by congregational government. That is, each congregation is, as it were, a law unto itself. Historically, this was one of the hallmarks of the Dissenters. The British House of Commons had passed a statute in 1662 called the Act of Uniformity: it insisted upon the re-establishment of the Church of England in all its powers, and public worship had to be based on the Book of Common Prayer and its doctrine accepted. The non-Conformists would have nothing of this: no bishops, no hierarchy. Baptists held tenaciously to a belief in the priesthood of all believers, which meant that in a religious sense, Jack was as good as his master. Gatherings into a congregation of Baptists were independent of all other gatherings. Of course congregations had beliefs and procedures in common, but the governance of these individualist congregations was in the hands of the members, and not in some hierarchical body or synod. Still today in any union of Baptist churches, you will find a range in congregational attitudes from the literalist fundamentalist to the theologically radical. That I was an academic meant that the right wing of the union of churches would have nothing to do with me, would never call on me. The left wing in Victoria was much, much weaker in influence and opportunities for me as a layman to teach and preach, which I thought I did best, were very limited. The two clear curves of the outline of the fish were blurring. I entered a period of religious loneliness. We found a congregation where we were theologically comfortable, but after some years the minister resigned and was surprisingly replaced by a conservative: we moved to another congregation. Symbolic of my problem was the fact that to get to this new church I had to pass no less than four other Baptist churches.

There was, however, a positive effect from being an academic. I developed a relationship with the Baptists' Theological College, Whitley College within the University of Melbourne, tutoring there, sat on its governing council, had encouraging conversations with its lecturers. My loneliness was mollified a little.

Within the Faculty of Education I had set up the first course in the country dealing with the non-government school sector, for this had become a consuming interest of mine and the subject of my doctoral dissertation. This meant that I spent an increasing amount of my professional time establishing relationships with the so-called 'church schools', Anglican, Roman Catholic and all the rest. My concerns were sociological: I wanted to examine what I came to call the life-style of these schools, which included the place of religion in their functioning. I was known to have sympathy with the religious basis of the schools and access to them became easy. As I reflect upon this period, I realise that I crossed what had been a great divide into the Catholic world and some of the best things I did were with the people in Order schools: the Christian Brothers, the Loreto Order, the Jesuits. I became less and less lonely. The fish was coming back into focus.

But it all wasn't without some deep unease. I'm now in my forties. I'm over halfway through my allotted span of years. Sometimes life makes no sense at all. I do things and think things that I know are shameful and they hang to me like shreds torn from my clothes by brambles. I blunder about in the secret world of my searching. It gets dark and I wonder where the way out is. I want to wrestle some honour, some constancy out of the snatching of the undergrowth. Specifics make me bleed. I grasp at the general, because that's safer. I try it in a poem I call 'Truth Comes Slow Like Starlight':

Over suburban acres of tilted tiled roofs
And the creeping of headlights
Around the curves of hills and valleys,
Over the bushfire-glow of the city's filament,
Stars prick their whiteness, blueness, redness,
And swoop around (but how imperceptibly)
Conical sections drawn in disbelief
In some dim astronomical pre-history.

Over the dim acres of all my dreams' roofs
And the uncertain brake-lights
Behind me as I lean around the banked turns
That take me further from men,
Truth in its whiteness, blueness, redness
Slips through clouds and the rhythmic swipe
Of misty rain on my windscreen. Yet
The parabola of its passage often escapes me.

The whiteness, blueness, redness, gradually become clearer through the atmosphere's diffraction my doubt and timidity set up. I've been here before, of course, and escaped. I'll escape again.

But there was always something. In the late 1970s there appeared a growing number of so-called 'Christian schools'. There were two kinds, the Accelerated Christian Education Schools and the Christian Community Schools. It was a source of intense embarrassment to me to know that the ACE schools had a regime based on a program developed by the fundamentalist Southern Baptists in the United States and that the Christian Community Schools were largely developed in New South Wales by local Baptist Churches. The latter grouping was legally incorporated and the resultant company had a Confession of Faith to which all members had to give assent. The first item in the Confession ran

> We believe in the Divine inspiration, the infallibility and supreme authority of the Old and New Testaments in their entirety and that the Holy Spirit so moved the writers that what they wrote are authoritative statements of truth for all matters of faith and conduct.

I was suddenly back with my father's Brethren family, back with my Campaigners friends. Will this fundamentalism never die? There were twelve statements of faith like this in the company's document. The tenth said

> We believe in the actual existence of Satan who is the father of all evil and opposed to God although ultimately subject to the purposes of God and destined to be confined forever to Hell.

This was medieval. It brought to my mind what I'd read about the fifteenth-century miracle plays in York and Wakefield and other places: the wheeled stages going the rounds of a town's streets, with a great black hole for Hell and a Devil in red with horns and a tail tempting the gaping-mouthed peasants. I couldn't or didn't want to believe that outside some minor crackpot Pentecostalist sect anyone could subscribe to this, but behind it all were Baptists, my co-religionists.

I was getting tired of this. 'Your Baptist friends are at it again,' my university colleagues used to say when the denomination had been reported in the press as saying something illiberal or foolish. When people would say to me, 'But you're not a Baptist?' I had a stock reply: 'In this century there have been two well-known Baptists, Billy Graham and Harvey

Cox, and I'm up the Harvey Cox end.' Then I'd often have to explain who Harvey Cox was, a liberal theologian with a social conscience. It was being borne in on me that the Baptist thing in my life was the Church. Did I want to be a part of that Church?

Salvation seemed always at hand, whenever depression seeped into my thinking about religion. Every seven years university academics took by right a sabbatical year, usually overseas, to consult with other academics in their field, to write, to conduct research. I spent sabbaticals at the University of Cambridge.

Cambridge kept me in the church or at least in the company of believers. I'm sure it was because my mind there was clear of administrivia, not having to remember this, remember that, reply to him, write to her, and I was able to read and think almost effortlessly. As a family we attended the Baptist Church in St Andrews Street. Our minister was Rev. Arthur Jestice, a rather fey man but with an acute intelligence who was a regular preacher in the chapels of the Cambridge colleges. Arthur's sermons were sharp with insight, demanding, thought-provoking; he seemed to belong in a university town. Often we attended services at night at Great St Mary's, the University Church, and the pews were crammed with undergraduates wanting to hear from people like the Right Reverend Trevor Huddleston, Father Harry Williams, Rt. Reverend Hugh Montefiore, the Dean of Guildford, C. Day Lewis, Professor David Martin, John Stott, Rector Emeritus of All Souls Langham Place, John Hick. A couple of times I heard Professor C.F.D. Moule, Lady Margaret Professor of Divinity, preach occasional sermons in St Bene't's: despite a high-pitched almost wavering voice, he had about him an impregnable certainty. Once I audited a course entitled 'Seventeenth Century Prose: the Bible as

Literature', given by (I met and spoke with him at last) T.R. Henn. The breadth of his knowledge and understanding was immense and he treated matters of belief with a fine courtesy.

We were in Cambridge in 1977 at the time of 'The Myth of God Incarnate' controversy. The ferment on radio and television and in newspapers was wonderful; here, obviously, was something that was important to a lot of people. In the Cambridge corner was Don Cupitt, Dean of Emmanuel College. One point he made as I understood him was that Jesus was the mind of God and that the doctrine of the incarnation unified things that Jesus in his message kept in ironic contrast with each other. Cupitt came in for a lot of flack, but as our dear Arthur Jestice said to us once: 'The trouble with Don is that people can understand what he is saying.' Cupitt went on to notoriety with a BBC television series in the early 1980s called 'The Sea of Faith: Christianity in Change', which became a book that has spawned a heretical group of ordained churchmen who believe that religion is a human creation and so is God. It *is* Cupitt's trouble: people do understand what he's saying.

Cambridge was also for me a great place for second-hand books, especially theology and biblical studies; I even found a copy of Harvey Cox's *God's Revolution and Man's Responsibility*. That was Cambridge for me, revolution and responsibility.

Sabbatical leaves were good for us as a family. The first one saw us in the northern summer drifting across Europe with a campervan and tent to obvious places like Paris and Salzburg and less obvious ones like Ljubljana in what was then Yugoslavia, and Martin Luther's Wurms. We were arrested in Italy as a result of mistaken identity, marvelled at the modern, sharply bright stained glass in the Swinglikirche in

Zurich, and were bitten alive by mosquitoes on the banks of the Loire River. The children got it into their heads that they wanted a Bavarian cow bell as a souvenir, and not one from a tourist shop. I could be firm as a father: I'd learned from my own. Late one afternoon I pulled up on a back road near a farmhouse. 'Off you go.' I said. 'You want a bell, you negotiate for it. You've got enough German between you. We'll wait here.' In fifteen minutes they were back, grinning, bearing a large bell attached to a very smelly leather collar. 'And the farmer gave it to us for nothing,' they gasped.

We had one of our near misses on this trip. Our rather overwrought van had managed in sunshine with infinite patience to negotiate the three great passes in the Swiss Alps, Furka, Susten and Grimsel, with their dozens of hairpin bends. On our final descent, we reached the floor of the valley just as it came on to rain. Our cases were on the roof rack without cover and I made to slow down, but the brake pedal went straight to the floor. Only tyre friction brought us eventually to a halt. Ten minutes earlier while up the mountain we'd have probably all have been killed. I thanked God: I couldn't help it. Was it a sign, I wondered to myself.

During our time in Europe Peter was working on a Queensland cattle station as part of his farm management course. We had only David and Jane with us: they got on well and went together to France twice. David then set off to research (his word) Byzantine churches in Serbia with money saved by cleaning toilets in Cambridge's St Catherine's College. He lived from hand to mouth in Rome and apart from the odd postcard we spent most of the two months he was away worrying about him.

This second visit to Cambridge gave us memories enough for a lifetime. We rented a house in the tiny village of Coton (a medieval church, a general store and post-office) a short ride from town along a cycle path across open fields. Flurries of snow when we first arrived gave way to daffodils and crocuses and the orchard trees burst into blossom. As a family we went to concerts in college chapels, in the Senate House and, several times, in the Norman vastness of Ely Cathedral. Jane's French pen-friend Jacqueline came to stay and we had a succession of Australian visitors. David and Jane attended the Folk Music Festival in the summer. David audited a Fine Arts course at the university and researched for his honours thesis the architectural history of the interesting West Front of Peterborough Cathedral. Jane followed a Year 10 program from the Correspondence School. We had letters and tapes from Peter who turned twenty-one that year. When he wrote about Aboriginal stockmen, his cattle dog called Bruce and being dragged through the dust by a rearing horse, we realised how far from Australia we really were.

Professionally my faith was never far from what I was doing. In 1977 in Cambridge a Wolfson College Visiting Fellowship gave me the space and calm to write a book for English teachers. It was *The Water and the Wave: an approach to literature in secondary schools* and I wrote it in a Department of Education room with a year's view of a beautiful plane tree. In the opening chapter of the book, 'The Search for Beauty', I tried to explore the very human wish to make beautiful things, to reach a point of awareness of that beyond ourselves. The second chapter, 'Experiencing the Real', after an examination of the notion of perception, concludes with a claim that owning or developing a sense of wonder is essential in coming to an experience of reality. There's no God or Jesus in these chapters but I believe they are informed by a religious sense. When I write of my sense of vocation, it's this that I mean, that like a religious, everything I do is done, as a religious would say, 'under God'.

I loved teaching and, if I can believe the testimony of former students, I was good at it. I never saw it other than as a vocation and the sense of a calling kept breaking into my classrooms. There was always the technical stuff like phrases and tenses. I was good at that: I brooked no nonsense. I insisted on English usage being *right*, upon structures holding together. But there was always another side to what I was doing. I always wanted to enlarge the view of the world my students had, to coerce them into experiences (Kurt Hahn's phrase) that they may otherwise have missed.

I remember a group of Sixth Formers I had at Eltham College in London. They were the Science Set, very bright, sharp: they would go on to Oxford and Cambridge and University College, London. The school insisted they undertake a program of humanities to balance the intensity of their science subjects, and the responsibility for that was mine. I did a study with them on Elizabethan and Jacobean scientific discovery and geography and its influence on the metaphysical poets, concluding the year with T.S. Eliot's *The Waste Land*.

I recall vividly the boys' response to the lines about 'the third who walks always beside you': we talked together about the way hope and doubt often come upon each other and what if things we've been brought up to believe in are not there? Is the land waste? They were deep moments.

I loved that experience (which committed teachers all know) of seeing comprehension and recognition flowering on the faces of students who struggled, been cajoled into understanding. It often happened with me with Ted Hughes' poem, 'Thistles', when finally the cycle of nature idea dawned on a class. I would see the nod of realisation around the room as I pointed out the lines in James McAuley's poem 'Terra Australis'

And who shall say on what errand the insolent emu
Walks between morning and night on the edge of the plain,

and by re-reading them show how the rhythm exactly captures the forward-jerking gait of the emu. Quiet reflectiveness would settle over a class during a discussion of how Vance Palmer's 'The Rainbow Bird' reminds us that difference is often painful.

One of the classes I took during my university lecturing was at Melbourne's University High School: this was a group (at my request) of middling ability but, as it turned out, of great sensitivity. I wanted to explore the possibilities of drama in the classroom, as distinct from a specialist drama space, so I could talk to my Education students about it. I had chosen Shakespeare ('Shakespeare's boring, my brother says') and *Julius Caesar*. With the class I used the old trick of giving groups of three or four some twenty lines of text to express in contemporary English, slang, even, and rehearse those lines to get the feeling right. Then the groups would revert to the play's lines, maintaining the emotion of the modern English. After a fortnight I chose randomly some groups to make a presentation. One of the groups had only two actors, a boy and a girl, and I can't remember how that happened. However, this pair was to do about thirty lines from Act 2 where Portia tries to find out what's bothering her Brutus: 'Dear my Lord,/Make me acquainted with your cause of grief'. These two fifteen-year-olds stood on the dais in front of the blackboard in this almost Dickensian classroom and spoke not their lines but their selves. When this Portia, risen from her knees, moved away from Brutus and, head over her shoulder, said,

Dwell I but in the suburbs
Of your good pleasure? If it be no more,
Portia is Brutus' harlot, not his wife,

I thought my heart would burst. Did I just talk to my wife 'sometimes'? I thought. Was my marital relationship 'as it were in sort or limitation'? This young Portia had touched a nerve. All I could do (no teacher would dare do this any more) was lay my hands on her shoulders (could she see the tears in my eyes?) and say, 'Wonderful. Thank you. Go to your seat now.'

10. Big Ideas

Dorothy had always been the devoted wife and mother, always dutiful. She had enjoyed our time in school boarding houses, loved living in the school grounds with students passing by, accompanying school Gilbert and Sullivan performances and tending to the needs of small boys in their first year away from home. She had typed all my theses although she was not a trained typist, sat up in bed with me late at night placing Education students in schools for their teaching practice. She carried, however, a regret from childhood: she'd always, from as long as she could remember, wanted to be a teacher. As a child she would line up younger children and teach them. When in her teens the time came for her to choose a career there was only one that interested her. Teaching. Her father, arguing from the fact that he had cousins who were all teachers and all middle-aged spinsters, refused to allow her to go to university or teachers' college. Her mother, a Scot, had only an aunt and two cousins as relatives in Australia and he didn't want his daughter sent to some country school away from the family. There were three brothers still to be educated and with great reluctance Dorothy left the Presbyterian Ladies' College that she loved. She became a research librarian.

When our children were settled in their schools, Dorothy offered herself as a Religious Instruction teacher with the Council for Religious Education in Schools. There was a short course given to those wanting to teach, and she began teaching in two nearby primary schools and loved it from the moment she entered the classroom. It wasn't much, it wasn't quite what she wanted, but it was better than nothing. At least she was getting to teach.

After some years of this, Dorothy volunteered (she was always volunteering) to also help out in the Junior School Library of our daughter's school, Methodist Ladies' College: the library stock needed cataloguing and Dorothy had the skills. One day, late in 1979, the principal, David Loader, asked her if she would like to teach Religious Education in the Senior School. She demurred. It would take up a lot of time, she wasn't sure if she could do it, she would think about it. But she dismissed it. Without formal qualifications she knew it was useless even to think any more about it.

Some weeks later David Loader approached her again. You haven't sent in an application for the R.E. job, he said. She didn't even know the job had been advertised. Loader then sent her an application form. As well as personal details it asked for qualifications and experience. None of my experience has been formal, she said. And thought: 'This is bizarre.' But out of courtesy she wrote a letter explaining her situation and thought that was the end of it. But no. She was called up for an interview. Don't worry, I said. Relax. They'll only ask straightforward questions. Nothing to it. You've read a lot of theological stuff, heard fine lecturers and preachers, it'll be all right. She told me afterwards that the first question she was asked was: 'Mrs Hansen, how would you begin to develop a sense of religious awareness in Year 11 girls?' After the interview we met for a cup of coffee. In tears she told me she had made a mess of the interview and would never try for a teaching position again.

It just so happened that we were going out that evening to a College of Education dinner. The last thing Dorothy wanted to think about was schools and education. At six o'clock the telephone rang. It was David Loader offering her the job. This was a remarkable example of instinct prevailing over formal qualifications. Some years earlier the Chief Education Officer for the West Riding of Yorkshire, Sir Alec Clegg, had visited Australia. Talking with Dorothy at a dinner he had said that he would certainly put her in charge of a school in England. At the time she thought he was just flattering her.

Over the summer before her first school year began, Dorothy read and read and read. We bought a new set of shelves to accommodate her books on religious education, theology, Buddhism, Jewish culture. Dorothy held me by the hour, late into the nights, as we wrestled some plain sense out of concepts like love, grace and hope. With her four Year 10 classes she was to follow the school's program of a study of world religions but for the senior girls, she was devising her own approaches to themes like family, future careers, death, social issues, and issues of Christology. She worried away at lesson plans and was determined that only the best would do.

It was 1980. Peter was already assistant manager on a Riverina sheep property, David was the country's youngest public regional art gallery director and Jane was doing first year Arts and aiming for an honours degree in modern languages. I'd been elected a Fellow of the Australian College of Education and felt good about what I was doing. It was one of the happiest periods of our lives together and I have a photograph to prove it, taken by a friend, of the five of us laughing together in the back garden.

No period in my religious life was quite like this one. Dorothy continually raised questions to do with her belief system and involved me as a sounding-board. Whether I liked it or not I was forced to confront what *I* believed, what *I* thought about God the Father, about Creation-myths, about the resurrection of Jesus. And Dorothy came to see that often the way in for her senior girls was through poems, plays, and novels. You have to supply these, she said. What can I use to illustrate courage, pain, fear, joy?

We had both reached the stage of seeing the whole of existence in a variety of religious terms. I would read a poem new to me and if it was at all amenable to a religious gloss, then that's how I would see it. The world itself was suffused with a wonder that had its origin in a religious awareness. So we went at it together, Dorothy and I, drawn closer by the common need to know and experience.

I watched sometimes amazed as the number of her books grew, Mircea Eliade's *The Sacred and the Profane*, Hans Kung's *On Being a Christian*. Paul Tillich's *The Dynamics of Faith*. There was a whole shelf on Judaism, there was Simone Weil and Viktor Frankl, Carl Jung and Peter Berger, Fletcher's *Situation Ethics* John Hick's *Faith and Knowledge* and Jean-Claude Barreau's *The Religious Impulse*. Dorothy's books became my books, for she was always reading bits out to me at the meal-table or in bed. Even now, two decades later, I'll take down something from her bookcase and, thumbing through it, find underlinings and comments in the margin in her handwriting, and remember the times we talked together about faith issues.

Finally I owe a lot to my father, and remote though he was, he took me out of a narrow religious culture before I got locked into it, and enlarged my apprehensions of the whole world of the spirit. However, had it not been for my wife's passionate concern to prepare herself as best she could for her Religious Education career, I'm not sure that I would have read so intently and intensely in the rather rambling fields of belief. Her focus gave me a focus.

During the 1970s and early 1980s I was on the School

Speech Night circuit. That is, I was regularly the speaker at end-of-year prize-givings, at a small country high school here, at a large private school there. The year that David Loader offered Dorothy a job at Methodist Ladies' College was our daughter Jane's final year at the school. Dorothy kept a day book in which she recorded particular events or copied out quotations that appealed to her. In that day book she described Jane's Leavers' Chapel Service:

> As the procession came down the chapel aisle I saw Jane leading with a lighted golden candle in her hand. Later in the service her description of how she had grown during the year was very moving and Ian was so proud. There was a lump in Jane's throat but she didn't let it show.

Three days after the chapel service was the MLC Speech Night and I was the invited speaker. When Jane came across the platform to receive her academic prizes from me, she went up on tiptoe and kissed me.

I could have got stale as a believer. I was now in my fifties, a dangerous age. Dangerous because men, with their tendency by sex to be uni-directional, are content to let things plod along. Having reached the big five-oh men often believe they've arrived. They probably have, in their occupations, in careers, and enjoy some position of seniority in their places of employment, and become not a little self-satisfied. For lay churchmen it's a particularly risky time of life. They look back to their twenties and thirties when their religious beliefs settled, and feel there's nothing more for them to do about where they stand in relation to God and the world. For many, the fifties are fallow years. The sixties are when it all happens: old friends get seriously ill, children realise they've made a mistake in marrying the person they're married to, retirement looms darkly, elderly parents die or are confined to nursing homes. But the fifties are when many rest on their oars, relax, become intellectually quiescent. A dangerous age.

I was fortunate. There was all this excitement going on with Dorothy, all this zealous interest which she shared with me in coming to real terms with matters of belief. There was also something in my temperamental and intellectual equipment that saved me from passivity. By temperament I was reflective, a legacy of my polio. By training I was experienced in reading and in analysing my reading. I had at least some of the skills of the literary critic. Books didn't frighten me. I liked books.

So in my fifties I read works like Paul Clifford's *Interpreting Human Experience*, Paul van Buren's *The Secular Meaning of the Gospel* and Rabbi Kushner's honest little books, *When Bad Things Happen to Good People* and *When All You've Ever Wanted Isn't Enough*. I read Daniel Jenkin's *Beyond Religion*, John Macquarie's *An Existentialist Theology* and the Australian Bruce Wilson's *The Human Journey: Christianity and Modern Consciousness*. But nothing could compare in all my reading from then and since with what I gained from two books, no, two particular ideas from two books.

The first book was Sam Keen's *Apology for Wonder* (1969), and the idea from it which made a real difference in me was the distinction he made in a religious context between the Apollonian and the Dionysian way of being. Classical Greek culture revered the Apollonian ideal of moderation. Life was to be formal and remain within the bounds of accepted social mores. Anything that would threaten the divine order of reason was highly suspect. Then, argued Keen, Christianity came into the ancient world as a rebellion against the stifling domination of Apollo. Not only did Christianity set itself against the Greek idea that history was orderly and was ruled by fate, but it fought also against the Jewish idea that life should conform to religious and ceremonial laws. Christianity emerged as the advocate for Dionysus. The virtues of the Dionysian way of living were enthusiasm, spontaneity and a continuing vision of possibilities: Dionysus gets rid of awareness of the limits that seem to govern existence. Boundaries and laws 'are dissolved in the endless flux of existence'.

Now it has to be admitted that as Christianity developed its culture in the West it lost sight of its Dionysian origins. It went on to produce a new legalism, a strong sense of the importance of tradition and strictures that allowed for nothing new. Within mainstream churches one need only compare a regular worship service in an Anglican cathedral with a service in one of the Greek or Russian Orthodox branches of the Church: in the former, order, careful dignity, calm; in the latter, colour, casualness, movement, enthusiasm.

I found this idea provocative. The early church certainly fought against legalism, for Jesus had no time for the crippling religious laws that beset Israel. Against most severe criticism, for example, he gave himself to the sick on the Sabbath. But, I asked myself, whatever happened to joy in the churches? And I didn't mean the religious extravagances of Pentecostalism or the abandon of the Afro-American congregations as I heard them on some of my jazz records. What about joy in *my* church? Where was the Dionysian thread that history had woven in the tapestry of Christian belief and practice? I'm not such an iconoclast that I would smash the image of God's people meeting reverentially in silent prayer, communing mystically with the Other. I just want to feel that there is some balance between Apollonian and Dionysian ways of being religious.

Where I have a problem with Dionysus in the church is the enthusiasm that is a mask for an unwillingness to think things through. What passes for joy can often be ersatz, inauthentic, thin.

Sam Keen gave me a picture of the Church, a way of looking at belief that had not occurred to me before. For me, it was a kind of big idea.

More than ten years later, I came across another one. It was in a study by John Dominic Crossan called *The Historical Jesus: The Life of a Mediterranean Jewish Peasant* (1991). With a fine clarity, Crossan paints a convincing picture of Roman Mediterranean social ways of being. In the Roman Mediterranean, there was a web of patronage and clientage. That is, in any transaction between two citizens, one was left with some kind of responsibility to the other. If I do you this favour or I put this piece of business your way, then you owe me. I can call upon you at some future time and exact from you some favour in return. Cash for favours is not admissible because cash cuts off the imbalance of owing something and hence closes off the relationship for the future. There is, however, a disparity in power between patron and client, and patronage is almost certain to be exploitative and even repressive. And to facilitate the deals struck, a middle man or broker plays most often an intermediary role.

It's all more complicated than I have summarised here, but the point about the message brought by Jesus was this: in the Kingdom, there were to be no more deals. This must have sounded in his hearers' ears like a thunder clap. They were part of this culture of patron, client and broker. They did nothing, they accepted nothing without having to consider the consequences. Now this preacher proclaimed (that was the word for it) that in the Kingdom of God there were to be no deals. Access to God's love and compassion and power was free and untrammelled: men and women could thankfully embrace the unmediated presence of God. No more deals, Jesus was saying. This idea I found wonderfully satisfying, for it underlined for me the utter freedom of the gospel, the openness of all that good news.

I suppose these two ideas were seminal for me because they came from within the context of the story of Jesus and of the church. I'd always wanted to know where things came from, both words (I loved chasing the origins of words like 'bunkum' and 'eavesdrop') and also ideas, and here were two ideas that, because I knew where they'd come from, I could internalise and make mine.

What I've set down here about my reading, seems to suggest that my religious awarenesses are simply intellectual. When I recall stages in my belief-journey, they appear to be marked by mental notions, by ideas, by an Apollonian world-view, as Sam Keen might say. What about *feeling*? Do I *feel* about my religious position?

Well, yes. I can find myself in tears listening to a CD of a Haydn quartet, I can weep quietly at a concert or a recital or a poem or a line in a play or hanging up after a phone call from a grandchild. I have this sense of awe and wonder, a marvelling at how wonderful life and existence can be. I've sat mid-week in winter in King's College Chapel in Cambridge, in a congregation of worshippers numbering five, and heard the choir's purity of sound echoing down the centuries and thought my heart would burst. I've sat in San Marco in Venice and watched the incense reaching in silver clouds towards the sparkling golden dome and felt it catching my own private prayers up to some heaven. I've sat in midsummer in a stifling corrugated-iron church in a straw-coloured Gippsland paddock where the people of God only meet once a month, and watched the offering being received while a wheezy pedal-organ is played inexpertly, and I've loved this handful of country folk at worship.

I feel very deeply about the nearness to me of Jesus. It's not some metaphysical imagining, some psychic awareness with no basis in reality. I simply feel it. Don't ask for rationality here: this isn't where the rational operates. One of the deepest philosophical and theological questions is whether reality is surrounded by something or nothing. If it's surrounded by something, we have, as it were, to give a face to it. For me it's the face of Jesus. Forget Carl Jung and Paul van Buren and Daniel Jenkins and all the rest of my reading: to me it finally comes down to *believing* in something surrounding reality, something beyond self. I can't separate believing and feeling. I *feel* about the humanity of Jesus, I *feel* that the gospel is mine. And I'm going to have to explain. And I'm sorry if that explanation sounds suspiciously like a sermon.

In the days of his flesh (to use a phrase from my father's generation), Jesus offered to his disciples an intimate companionship. In Luke's account of his life, there is a record of two parables told to the disciples alone. They are two of the most puzzling of the stories Jesus told. One is about an apathetic neighbour in bed with his children and not wanting to be disturbed; the other concerns an unrighteous judge who hears a woman's case only because she wears him out with her constant nagging. These are whimsical illustrations of the nature of God, tongue-in-cheek. The stories, insightful for the disciples, not for the general public, are making the point that prayer is no swift and easy way of achieving what you want, nor is it a magical guarantee against trouble. Jesus was a companionable leader. Good Jews all, the disciples knew the Hebrew story of the three Israelites flung into the burning, fiery furnace and how they walked through it without so much as the smell of the smoke on their clothes. It's not history, it's a tale, like the one about the apathetic neighbour, a symbolic tale and parable for the disciples' times. Because, in the story, there walked with the Israelites 'one like unto the Son of God'. The disciples themselves walked with a divine companion, however hard they sometimes found that to believe. For each of them Jesus was always there, helping them to transmute the way they met circumstances. He never claimed he could save them from the waters but offered something infinitely greater: 'When you pass through the waters, I'll be there, too'.

There's a story my father could well have told: it comes from the trenches of France in World War I. A soldier asks permission to bring in from No Man's Land his grievously wounded mate. The young officer says, 'If you want to go, then go, but it'll probably not be worth it. He's more than likely dead by now, you'll probably get killed and you'll be throwing your life away for nothing.' The soldier is insistent and climbs over the parapet and is gone. Forty-five minutes later he staggers back to the trench with his mate limp over his shoulders. He's been hit twice and falls into the trench exhausted. The officer snaps at him, 'I told you it wouldn't be worth it. Here you are, look, your mate's dead and you're seriously wounded.' The soldier looks up at him and says, 'Yair, but it was worth it. Know what he said to me when I got to him? He said, "I knew you'd come."'

For me, it's just like that. God, Jesus, Spirit, whatever the presence is, it's there and I know it will come to me in my No Man's Land. God, which will do for an inclusive name, is for me not only the *logos* of being, that is the structures of reality, but also the *telos* of being, that is, the end, direction and purpose of existence. I can only *feel* this. I don't have the philosophical or theological equipment to argue it through.

I simply sense it, that Presence, that Coming. The Coming sustains me.

Believers talk about 'the presence of God' and you'd be hard pressed to define what they mean when they use the phrase. 'God's in my garden,' says one. 'God's in my lover's eyes,' says another. 'God is always by my side.' 'God walks with me.' What's this all mean? That for believers, God in their lives is a constant presence? I just can't see it like that. God is coming. God in *my* life is a sporadic presence.

There was a time when for all men and women God was everywhere and inescapable: in the Middle Ages, God was everywhere to be seen. At the centre of any settlement, city, town or village was the church. People saw the church every day, passed by it, entered it, read the Bible stories in stone carvings or stained glass week by week. The hand of God was in everything, birth, death, sorrow, joy: God was in art and music and philosophy. Now, however, in the third millennium, it's very difficult to cultivate the idea of the presence of God. The self-improvement industry tells us that we can do it all ourselves if we try hard enough, so we don't need God. For a certain kind of believer, God is still seen everywhere. These believers see God in a bus or in a post office or in the supermarket but to 'see' God like this requires a particular mind-set or emotion-set. On the other hand, there are numerous references in the literature of Christian mysticism to what is called 'the dark night of the soul'. The phrase was first coined by St John of the Cross, perhaps the most famous of the Christian mystics. Nowadays the phrase is used as a metaphor for periods of peculiar emptiness and depression in the religious life – often people use it at times of bereavement or fear. However, in the writings of St John of the Cross himself it's used to refer not to experiences of exceptional spiritual deprivation but to the everyday life of faith. For St John of the Cross, 'night' was an appropriate metaphor for normal Christian experience.

I wish someone had told me that life would not be happiness tinged with sadness but rather sadness illumined with some joy. Life is a vale of tears, the Victorian hymn writers told us, and we thought it was a bit of a joke. It was a bleak view from lugubrious sabbatarians. But I now think perhaps they were right after all. I remember my early life as a Christian believer had some darkness (my father's response to my conversion, for example) but mostly my living was lit by a vivid sense of God's presence. However welcome those God-moments were, they didn't last and I don't think they were meant to last. Over most of my religious journey, I've had to travel blind or, as Scripture would put it, walking by faith and not sight.

I've often had a sense of God's absence, an awful empty feeling that there is only me. People in the first flush of glorious commitment can't imagine this happening, but it does. Things have crowded in on me, stresses of all kinds. I've been battered by events in the lives of my children. There have been problems, sometimes of my own making, and an enervating *ennui* has suffused all my responses. I haven't been bothered to try and make sense of anything because God wasn't there, it seemed.

This 'absence of God' notion is a recurring theme in much twentieth-century literature. It's not only found in writers on the Holocaust: it's also in those with a Christian upbringing against which they've rebelled and who keep turning back, despite themselves, to questions of the reality of God. They don't deny God's existence: they protest against his absence. They don't say, 'There is no God': they say, 'Where are you, God?' It's there in Franz Kafka and Samuel Beckett and Graham Greene – the God who appears to be hiding. Then I find that encouraging observation of Karl Barth's: 'What God has revealed is the hiddenness of God'. It's a mind-spinning notion, that. It's something not only to think but also to feel, the presence of the hidden. A fine book on the nature of God, Rudolph Otto's *The Idea of the Holy*, suggests that the Holy, the numinous, is *mysterium tremendum*, a great mystery which defies human understanding but demands human acceptance. For all his hiddenness, God *is*. Paradox on paradox. Jesus coming.

This is the point where the unbeliever gives up and says it makes no sense. Of course it doesn't make sense. Deep religious experiences are not meant to make sense, and if you haven't had one, you can't understand how beyond reason it all is. I remember once a religious group on the campus of my university advertising a forthcoming mission with the slogan, 'Give God a Piece of Your Mind'. I always tried to do that, to offer to God whatever intelligent processes there are in my head. But I also recognise that thinking is not enough. I've got to be prepared to be puzzled, and be honest enough to admit it. I've got to suspend rationality and feel, to confess susceptibility if need be. For me, God is and isn't, is present and absent, is revealed and hidden. That God seems sometimes not there, in my view, is no cause for self-accusation. I don't have to blame myself if in the dark night his presence is not palpable. That he's sometimes not there doesn't mean I'm abandoned. When I say I feel deeply about the nearness of Jesus, that incarnate God, I mean that there are moments in my living when I have in me an inexpressible confidence. I have to fall back upon traditional language and call that confidence the Spirit of God. It's the Spirit that is this Coming God.

Seratonin is a substance in the human body that helps determine our sense of well-being. It makes us feel alive and cheerful and positive; if we lack it we feel grey, depressed and negative. Now seratonin is activated by sunlight. Bright sunny days make us feel good, dark rainy days make us feel glum. No sunlight, no active seratonin and therefore no sense of well-being. It's a good metaphor for the religious life. The 'seratonin' activated by God's presence gives us well-ness rather than illness. That is why I dare to believe the Psalmist-poet when he says, 'The darkness and the light are both alike to Thee.'

11. 'It's a Parable, Dummy!'

The 1980s were good years for me professionally, perhaps peak years, if that phrase is not too grandiloquent. I was involved in the national and local politics of English teaching and I wrote regularly for journals. I was a member of the Council of Lauriston Girls' School, a well-known and highly regarded private school in Melbourne. In 1982 I was invited to teach a short course on the Australian short story at the University of Venice. The following year the Canadian Council of Teachers of English asked me to present a research paper at their annual conference held that year in Montreal. At that conference I was invited to present the opening keynote address at their next meeting in 1984.

My first visit to Canada was on my own. On the second visit Dorothy accompanied me, having been given leave from MLC to do so. We liked our Canadian hosts: Australians and Canadians have a lot in common. I was anxious to enlarge my reading and was introduced to a number of Canadian authors new to me. Alice Munro, the short story writer, struck chords. There was something familiar about the milieu she wrote from. When I realised what it was that I found resonating with me it came again to me how interconnected were so many aspects of my being. For Alice Munro's fictional world encompassed believers, churched and unchurched. On my return from Canada I was soon using incidents from her stories with discussion groups or even whole stories, like the wonderful 'Age of Faith'.

My centenary history of Melbourne's Camberwell Grammar School, *By Their Deeds*, was launched in 1986 by the then Governor-General, Sir Ninian Stephen. Later in that year we were invited to dinner at Government House in Canberra and to stay overnight.

I was asked to write the history of the Association of Heads of Independent Girls' Schools of Australia. I had too much on with teaching and other professional writing but suggested that Dorothy and I write it together. In the event, *Feminine Singular* was really Dorothy's book, but it established us as joint authors.

The year I turned sixty, 1989, I gave a paper at the University of East Anglia for Britain's National Association for the Teaching of English, and *Feminine Singular* was launched at the Sydney conference of heads of independent schools.

Despite all that has been set down, this book isn't a memoir in the accepted sense. I haven't told about riding my bicycle from Adelaide to Melbourne to see a girl I'd met at a youth conference and, being rebuffed, pedalling all the way back to Adelaide with an empty heart. I haven't told about my brief dalliance with militarism as a junior officer in the British Territorial Army in England and Germany, forced upon me by the threat of full-blown National Service, for I was a UK resident. I haven't told about trying in Melbourne to teach isolationist American college students about Australian literary culture or about trying in Portsmouth to train Iraqi electrical engineering students to write readable reports in English. I haven't told about one of my university colleagues, an educational psychologist, who'd published in a professional journal an article entitled, 'Minimal approach distant and peck frequency in domestic fowl'. There is a lot I haven't told because I've tried to edit my life down to those experiences that I believe have impinged upon my developing religious beliefs.

My father used to say that he didn't believe in the infallibility of The Church, nor in the infallibility of The Book. What he believed in was the infallibility of human experience.

The Church certainly isn't infallible if you're using an institutional definition of its nature. It's easy to disparage, even denounce that Church with the largest number of adherents, the Roman Catholic denomination. The Catholic Church is full of scandals, unimaginably wealthy, riddled with intrigue. At the turn of the millennium, countless parishes within its communion live in fear because of the ascendancy of a fundamentalist tradition in the Vatican. Powerful Catholics – Cardinals, Archbishops, politicians, businessmen in the *Opus Dei* movement – rail against contraceptives in Third World countries, against abortion and IVF programs, against homosexuals and against women presiding over the sacraments. The Catholic Church has been wracked by substantiated charges of child-abuse in orphanages and sexual abuse by parish priests and teaching brothers. It's a picture of an ungainly, insensitive monolith entangled in an uncompromising morality that leaves little room for grace. I feel so sorry for the Catholics I know who have to bear the weight of all this. *Ichthus*, the fish, is burdened by weeds and parasites clinging to its shape, making its clean outline ragged and fouling its environment like the carp of Australia's inland rivers.

In the mid-1970s Dorothy and I were guests at a Christian Brothers dinner. We told a headmaster at our table that we were bound in a few months for Cambridge via Rome. 'I can get you to a Papal audience if you like,' he said, 'because the Brother responsible for the audiences was a boy I taught once.' And so it was done, without fuss. In due course we presented ourselves at the papal apartments in the Vatican and were escorted past saluting Swiss Guards in their gorgeous gold, crimson and blue Michelangelo uniforms, along corridors and into the austere office of Brother Stan Maguire, a welcoming Australian. Stan's warmth and generosity were unbounded. If he thought to himself, 'Not another tourist couple from Australia, for heaven's sake,' he never showed it. Aware that our son studied Fine Arts, he took us through the papal collection of modern religious art, into obscure but beautiful Roman churches, into high-fashion boutiques in the Via Condotti for the sake of our teenage daughter. Stan's behaviour as host was pure grace.

And we got to Pope Paul's weekly audience. With 7000 others we waited in the grand swooping hall for the Holy Father to be borne down the central aisle on a portable throne to a vast stage. Clapping exploded like summer thunder; acres of white handkerchiefs waved and flapped in welcome. Despite ourselves, we became caught up in the charism of it all. Behind the Pontiff on the stage was a huge Raphael tapestry of the risen Christ striding out of the tomb, holding aloft a flag of victory.

After the ceremony of welcoming audience members in their own languages and a brief message of love and hope, the Pope pronounced a closing blessing. It was as though some electric charge passed from the tiny remote figure on the stage to the thousands of us in the cavernous hall. It was a sacred moment.

Almost twenty years later I had another intimate Catholic experience. The Society of Jesus had decided that the administration of their prestigious Xavier College in Melbourne would be vested in a governing council rather than it being in the hands of Jesuit priests only. The original council of priests and lay people was to have its members appointed by the then Provincial of the Order, Father Peter Steele. He was a member of Melbourne University's English Department, and so technically a colleague of mine. We knew each other, but not well, and he made me a member of that first Xavier Council. I was the only non-Catholic member. It was a courageous and also sensible appointment in that I could provide a point of view from outside the rather enclosed Catholic community. I was also well known to the then headmaster, Father Chris Gleeson.

Toward the end of our first year of operation, we held a weekend council retreat at the Jesuits' retreat house at Anglesea. On the Sunday morning a Mass was held and the officiating priest, Father Peter Quin, asked me to take the crumbed bread to the other priests present and to the lay members of Council. Next, I was the one to offer to each of the communicants the cup of wine. That was a remarkable display of openness, an exercise in freedom that deserved to be celebrated. Of course Peter Quin knew that I wasn't a Catholic. Of course he knew I was a Baptist. He probably knew (though I never asked him) of the Baptist tenet of the priesthood of all believers. Nevertheless, he was willing and prepared to have me (as a believer) handle in a Catholic setting the holy elements of the Eucharist and offer them to Catholic believers.

Just before my father began the Communion part of a church service, he would say, always, to the congregation, 'You are invited to the Lord's table, whether you are a member of this church, or some other church, or of no church. For it is the Lord who invites you.' That was something my Jesuit friends would understand.

I feel sorry for the Stan Maguires, the Peter Steeles and the Peter Quins, that they have to see the shortcomings of their Church paraded in banner headlines in newspapers. Their Church, The Church, is so fallible.

So is mine. Sociologists of religion provide figures suggesting that Baptists are doing pretty well. In my lifetime,

Baptists have doubled their numbers in Australia and represent the fastest growing of the mainstream denominations. Baptists have the highest percentage of regular church attenders – higher, that is, than even the Catholics. And there is, to me, that utterly remarkable statistic, that Baptists have the highest proportion of tertiary-educated Christians. These findings, however, mask a reality that causes me to despair. Many Baptist congregations are not unlike ghettos or comfortable snuggeries. For many members of Baptist churches, The Church is all that there is. All their friends are Baptists. All their leisure is taken in a Baptist context. The church for them becomes a sacred Rotary Club.

In his *Amusing Ourselves to Death*, Neil Postman has a devastating chapter entitled 'Shuffle off to Bethlehem'. Here he shows how the Church has become a part of the entertainment industry. His example is televised religion but what he says has ready application to the way some Baptists, particularly, see their church; The Church as a fun-parlour, with guitars and bongo drums and funky songs. A church service, not unfamiliar to Baptist people, might run like this: a cheerful hello to open proceedings, a song (hymns are *out*) with words on an overhead screen, a lengthy dramatisation of a Bible passage, jokey reports from representatives of various church committees (including a dining group and a netball team), more songs, a 'just and really' prayer, another song and at last a low level and undemanding sermon. (Someone actually said to me that he liked Reverend X's preaching 'because he's got so many funny stories'.) After the benediction, the band plays Christian rock as the congregation explodes into social chatter and retreats noisily to the laughter of the coffee bar in the foyer. Christianity is a serious and demanding religion, I would have thought. When it's delivered as easy and amusing, it's something else altogether.

The Baptist denomination has grown and continues to grow because in most of its congregations it offers simple faith that satisfies its adherents who want innocent certainties. There is little room for critical liberalism and this seems to be part of their response to a world of rapid social change. Baptists may not have to face being pilloried by the media over charges of paedophilia and sexual abuse, often a by-product of a celibate clergy. Nevertheless, Baptists are often sold short on issues of spiritual pain and doubt. And this despite having in Melbourne one of the finest theological colleges in the country.

My church keeps on letting me down. When I go to church, I want to encounter God, to experience the ineffable. I want to 'see Jesus'. I want to hear the deep calling to the deep. Thanks be to God, I can still do this in a Baptist church, occasionally. Too often, however, church-as-social club gets in the way, trying to accommodate every whim and taste a congregation can demand. My church has a problem. It wants to offer a comfortable place of worship for the baby-boomers and all the selfism they bring with them, it wants to attract somehow the largely uninterested Generation X, and the older generation of churchgoers has to try and deal with bongo drums in place of meditative silence.

If I'd been brought up Methodist or Congregationalist, I'd have been saying the same about the Uniting Church, where the environment seems little better for serious believers. The Anglican Church in Australia seems too often to attract negative media attention over matters of doctrine or ecclesiastical politics. The point I'm making is that the Church is not infallible. It lets people down.

Even the 'successful' Assemblies of God let people down. One of the Pentecostal groupings, the Assemblies of God congregations direct themselves to the under-40s, some of their centres producing CDs, tapes, books, posters and videos. A Queensland Christian rock group can earn nine million dollars in a year and what could be more successful than that? Yet the literalist fundamentalism on which these believers rely can sustain numbers of them for only so long and they leave dissatisfied. This is the fallible Church again.

It's easy for critics of the Church to focus on negatives It's easy to heap scorn upon the Church for its holier-than-thou attitude to AIDS victims and easy to forget that the Church was the first to establish hospices for AIDS patients. It's easy to snarl at a conservative politician and blame his religious upbringing for his attitudes. It's common sport among journalists to report upon the personal peccadillos and shortcomings of church figures like Martin Luther King Jr and Mother Theresa and, by implication, of the Church itself.

That scourge of fundamentalists, the American Bishop John Shelby Spong, has a phrase I find helpful. He writes, he says, for 'believers in exile'. He is concerned for Christians who find the Church a problem and find its traditional ways of thinking about the Kingdom uncomfortable. These believers refuse to abandon what they cling to as the reality of God, but they've been driven to sacrifice much of what the Church gave them. They feel exiled. So do I. I'm not going to give away the essences of my faith, but the Church is not doing much for me. I'm in a strange land and I don't know how to sing the Lord's song in it. Because (and Jack Spong, as his friends call him, doesn't take his idea this far) I have few people to talk to: I feel lonely and almost friendless in the Church. I have to seek out like souls and in the laity there aren't many of them to be found. I'm Spong's archetypal believer in exile.

There are times, I'm forced to confess, when in exile, something ineffable breaks in. Not so long ago, Dorothy and

I were attending a writers' conference in Canberra. Looking after us like a solicitous nephew was one of our boarders from Haileybury days who was researching at the Australian National University. 'On Sunday morning,' he said to us after we had reported a day of demanding presentations, 'we'll go to one of the Anglican churches: they are having a sung eucharist, I've heard.' So on the Sunday we went. I was not expecting much, but fortified myself with a sense of obligation and duty. The church was full, with worshippers of all ages and ethnicities. A simple liturgy was led by a woman priest who was full of restrained energy; she also presided over the eucharist. The preacher was a woman priest, too. Her sermon was on prayer, a measured and elegantly structured reflection, enriched by delicately expressed personal anecdote, but tough, demanding. Towards the end of the service as I stood in the aisle waiting to go forward to receive the bread and wine, and with the youthful choir singing S.S. Wesley's 'Thou Wilt Keep Him in Perfect Peace' a phrase came to me from, of all places, The Book. It was Peter's exclamation on the Mount of Transfiguration: 'It is good for us to be here.' That was it, in this Anglican church in Manuka. It was good for me to be there.

I can't explain this experience of the ineffable in terms of tradition. The Second Order of Holy Communion on p. 119 of *A Prayer Book for Australia* isn't my tradition, yet it moved me. I can't explain it in terms of community, either, for this wasn't my community. But I suppose on that particular morning I sensed I was part of a larger community of believers. I had a clear sense of being folded around by a presence that I was accustomed to call God. A mystery. *The* mystery.

I often find myself in a strange land and my sense of exile is deepened when I'm confronted with believers in the infallibility of The Book. I cannot accept that 'all scripture is given by inspiration of God, and is profitable for doctrine, for reproof, for correction, for instruction in righteousness'. The Apostle Paul is writing this to his young friend, Timothy. Paul is unwell and can see his life is drawing to a close. Of course he wants Timothy to be on the right track. Of course he is anxious for the health of the young man's soul, and all that'll be left for Timothy is Holy Scripture. But it's this '*all* scripture' that I jib at.

I have to return to the matter of my training. I'm not a theologian or a biblical scholar: if I'm anything in that line, I'm a literary critic (in its broadest sense). When, therefore, I come to examine The Book, I bring with me a whole set of literary, logical and historical understandings. One of The Book's difficulties for me is the rambling sequences of miracles through both the Old and New Testaments. Evangelical fundamentalists claim that, since 'all scripture is given by inspiration of God', *all* biblical miracles are a necessary part of Christian faith. My objection to the fundamentalist position is that it results in a kind of intellectual insecurity and that it is at bottom a misunderstanding of what faith really is.

A friend of mine from childhood days, Don Bowes, became a student of geology and later was appointed to a personal chair of Geology at the University of Glasgow. In our university days together, I once went with Don to the north-east of the Flinders Ranges in outback South Australia, where on a field trip he was researching a granitisation theory. I went as cook to the expedition. This experience of the world of science was fascinating for me. But there was in the Geology Department at that time a group of Christian believers who felt obliged to find in the creation story of Genesis a geological explanation. I forget the argument now, but it was seriously proposed that the biblical account could be made to mesh with geological periods. It seemed to me then and certainly does now that their view demanded of them a sacrifice of intellect, highly intelligent people though they obviously were.

A proper rationalist approach to miracle (how long was a creation 'day'?) is that miracle is scientifically impossible. The rationalist believer, therefore, must seek some explanation for miracle. Consider the feeding of the five thousand. A rationalist explanation, and I confess to have taken this view myself at a certain time in my development as a believer, goes like this. The disciples found the young lad with his packed lunch from home and persuaded him to share his loaf and fish with them. The nearby members of the crowd saw the boy sharing what he had and they began to share what they had: soon the whole multitude was sharing and at the end of the *al fresco* meal there were basketfuls of left-overs. Or consider the incident of the disciples who, after a night of fruitless fishing, are bringing their boat into shore. Jesus in the late dawn is standing on the shore of the lake and tells the disciples to let down their net on the other side of the boat. They pull up a huge catch. A miracle? No, because the low slant of the sun's rays is refracted by the water and Jesus can actually see a great shoal of fish moving towards the boat.

The rationalist view doesn't mean so much to me any more. I'm more inclined to the view that often the miraculous elements in the Gospel narratives particularly are legends from outside the Jesus-context. The headlong flight of the Gadarene swine over a cliff and into the lake is a local tale that became attached to the healing story. The water into wine is part of a cult myth of Dionysus. Or I'm inclined to think that the so-called miracles are metaphors from a literary-minded author.

Dom Crossan, the American biblical scholar, was once asked in a radio interview to comment on miracle:

> . . . what I notice . . . as a historian reading these stories, is that when you get to the so-called nature-miracles, the walking on the water, or the miraculous draught of fishes, they're done especially for the insiders, for the disciples. Usually healings and exorcisms are done for people along the road, as it were. Jesus doesn't come on the water to save the fishing fleet from Capernaum, he comes on the water to save the disciples. Now when I read that story, what it screams at me is: it's a parable, dummy, it's a parable. Don't you get it? If the leadership of the Church takes off in a boat without Jesus, it'll sink, it will get nowhere.

Healings and exorcisms I find acceptable: the nature-miracles I find at least questionable.

It's the layers in the Synoptic gospels that are the problem. There is the bottom layer that's Mark, the oldest, the nearest in time to the incidents it reports. 'Matthew' and Luke are expansions of Mark, and where they differ are clues to their own theology but of little historical value. Then there's another source for the Jesus-narrative, unknown to Mark but read by 'Matthew' and Luke, some of which was an oral tradition from the teaching and preaching of the primitive Church: this material is commonly called 'Q'. Further, 'Matthew' and Luke have special material which may well have come from other oral sources. So it's all very complex, this New Testament scripture.

The Old Testament is not without its difficulties, either. The strongest set of miracles relate to the prophets Elijah and Elisha. The Elijah story has, among others, the miracles of the unfailing cruse of oil, the feeding of the prophet by ravens and the slaying of two troops of soldiers by fire from heaven. The Elisha story has, among others, the feeding of a hundred men with twenty loaves, a mob of bears eating up mocking children and an axe-head floating in a stream. Then there's Joshua making the sun stand still (I call that poetry) and Jonah and the great fish (I call that parable). And there's the legendary heightening of historical events, like the collapse of Jericho's walls.

I'll put my position on The Book clearly by using my literary-critical training, taking as an example the Acts of the Apostles. When you read the life of the Jesuits' St Francis Xavier, you have two sources. First, there are the saint's personal letters and the accounts written by his fellow missionaries. In these records, there are no miraculous occurrences recounted. However, in later biographies, written much later, the saint's story is full of miracles. St Francis Xavier himself writes of the great difficulty he had in mastering the Japanese language, but in the later biographies he is portrayed as having picked up Japanese without formally having studied it and being able to speak it with such fluency that people thought he was Japanese. The miracle-stories grew around him: he made salt water fresh, he raised the dead, he caused an earthquake to bury a village, a crucifix he lost at sea in a storm was brought to shore in the claw of a crab. The further you get away from original sources, the more extravagant the narratives about religious figures become.

Let's apply this notion to the Book of the Acts. The book may be divided into two parts. There are the passages that are frequently referred to as the 'we' sections. These parts are in the nature of a first-person diary account of what was happening in the early missionary days of the Church: a bit like Francis Xavier's letters. In these 'we' sections there are 'miracles' which are explicable events. There's the story of the recovery of Eutychus' fall from a window (Acts 20:9–12), of Paul's avoidance of snakebite (Acts 28:3–6) and of the curing of a man suffering from dysentery (Acts 28:8). However, when we get away from these first-hand accounts and move into the other material that makes up the book, we are confronted with a set of marvels: a forty-year-old lifetime cripple is instantaneously healed (Acts 3: 1–8), Peter's shadow falling across the sick lining a street cures them all (Acts 5: 15–16) and when Peter is released from prison by an angel, his chains fall off and an iron gate opens to him 'of its own accord' (Acts 12: 6–10).

The Book is riddled with factual and moral inconsistencies. It's flawed. It's the revelation of God to men and women and that revelation begins with the Holy One of Israel, whose name is not to be spoken nor are images to be made of him. As The Book falteringly unfolds, God appears as unapproachable, unpredictable and impatient: the narrative brims with murders, adulteries and massacres. 'Given by inspiration?' Then The Book tells men and women about an inviting God, a God that seeks and forgives. I once saw the son of a young Jewish couple with his nose pressed to a window watching his father drive up. The little boy was crying in excitement 'Abba! Abba!' It was this kind of News that was Good: God as father, as Dad, intimate, loving, compassionate.

I believe God has intervened and does intervene in the human story giving men and women succour, judging them for their disobedience and pressing demands on them These interventions are for me the miracles of the Bible. They're not breaches of natural law but are occurrences which believers recognise as intimations of the Spirit of God. Faith recognises them as such.

There are two basic events in The Book that I believe are miracles, the Exodus and the Coming of Christ. They're foundation miracles, if you like, representing the old covenant and the new. They have attached to them what we may call ancillary miracles: the parting of the Reed Sea, the pillar of fire by night and the pillar of cloud by day, the water struck from the rock, the manna; the Virgin Birth, baptism, transfiguration, the empty tomb, the post-resurrection appearances. These ancillary miracles I either don't accept as fact or am agnostic about. They make little difference to the way I live my life here and now. The Exodus and the Coming do make a difference: they are foundational to what I believe, God Leading and God Coming.

So what does The Book do for me? There are things about it that I find interesting. For many believers, but not those in exile, the Virgin (a mistranslation) Birth is associated with the supernatural incarnation of Jesus – but virgin birth accounts didn't appear in Christian history until the 90s AD. Mark has no reference to Jesus having a magical birth and the only two times Mark mentions Jesus' mother, Mary, are neither of them flattering: Jesus was obviously an embarrassment to his mother. Tradition from The Book pictures Jesus as a simple village carpenter, making ploughs and yokes for oxen, yet if we are to accept the word the Greek Testament uses to describe his occupation, he was more likely a builder, though he was 'the son of a carpenter'.

I find many Old Testament stories powerful, like Jacob's wrestling at Peniel, and the Abraham and Isaac tale. Images there are forceful, like Jeremiah's parable of the potter and the clay and the psalmist making his bed in Hell and finding God there. Stories from the New Testament enrich any culture, not only a Christian one, like the temptation of Jesus in the wilderness and the conversation with the Samaritan woman at the well. There are striking images like the hen gathering her chickens under her wing and the sower casting seed as he walks.

There's no doubt The Book has the capacity to move people to wonderment and admiration. A New Age Buddhist writer friend of mine once rang me with a literary problem. He's never read the Bible, ever, and wanted some entry into the Christian belief system. Tell me about the Bible, he said. How did it come to be set down? What should I read first to get a feel for what Christians believe? I gave him, insofar as I could, an overview of the development of the scriptural canon and then suggested he read Mark's gospel straight off. A day or two later he rang again. 'I read Mark like you said,' he told me, 'And isn't it a fantastic story? I had no idea. I think it's absolutely marvellous.'

The Book does that to people. It does it to me. Certainly I admire and find helpful modern translations, but the romantic in me is drawn to the King James version when I'm reading looking for God.

And he said, Go forth, and stand upon the mount before the Lord. And, behold, the Lord passed by, and a great and strong wind rent the mountains, and brake into pieces the rocks before the Lord; but the Lord was not in the wind: and after the wind an earthquake; but the Lord was not in the earthquake: And after the earthquake a fire; but the Lord was not in the fire. and after the fire a still small voice.

He giveth power to the faint: and to them that hath no might he increaseth strength. Even the youths shall faint and be weary, and the young men shall utterly fall. But they that wait upon the Lord shall renew their strength; they shall mount up with wings as eagles; they shall run and not be weary: and they shall walk and not faint.

Seek ye the Lord while he may be found, Call ye upon him while he is near: Let the wicked forsake his way and the unrighteous man his thoughts; and let him return unto the Lord, and he will have mercy upon him; and to our God, for he will abundantly pardon. For my thoughts are not your thoughts, neither are your ways my ways, saith the Lord.

In the beginning was the Word, and the Word was with God, and the Word was God. The same was in the beginning with God. All things were made by him; and without him was not anything made that was made. In him was life; and the life was the light of men. And the light shineth in the darkness; and the darkness comprehended it not.

Peace I leave with you, my peace I give unto you; not as the world giveth, give I unto you. Let not your heart be troubled, neither let it be afraid.

These are indicators of the nature of God. Passage after passage in The Book signals the way to God: The Book is like a raised hand, index finger pointing. Literalists and fundamentalists tend to fix their gaze and their attention upon the pointing finger and don't look where the finger's pointing. The finger is fallible.

But while all my ferment of belief, begun that winter evening with Harry Bunday and my father long ago, was settling down into an integral acceptance in my belief system, much was happening in my personal and family life. I was entering my sixties and couldn't have guessed what lay ahead.

12. Paterfamilias

I used to say to my Education students that teaching was a conservative profession in the sense that we tend to teach the way we were taught. My Latin teacher at Norwood High was E.N. Pfitzner, tall, rather gangly, with wispy hair. He presented conjugations and declensions to us by semaphoring with his arms: right arm held high, 'amo'; right arm horizontal, 'amas'; right arm extended below to waist, 'amat'; left arm high, 'amamus'. He would rush into the room, stand before us with his left arm horizontal and cry, 'Spero – perfect tense' and we'd all be expected to answer, 'Speravitis'. This was the way *I* taught conjugations and declensions to junior classes.

I suppose I assumed it would be the way with parenting, that I would be the father my father was. But this was impossible. I wasn't my father at all. Once on the back verandah of the St Peters' manse Dad was squeezing a boil on the back of my neck – I got a lot of boils as a teenager – and when I cried out in pain he hit me across the face and hissed, 'Stand still!' I couldn't have done that to a son of mine. I wanted to project a New Testament father-image, rather than the fierce Old Testament image I was reared on.

I felt blessed in my children. They were physically whole and healthy. Could I have coped with a Down Syndrome child? I had a kind of horror of imperfection: I lived daily with my inadequate right hand and slightly emaciated right side. The thought of coping with a child who was crippled or retarded I always pushed away. In her final year of school, Jane had a friend (in the Bible class I took) called Steve, who during that year was operated on for a brain tumour. His hospital visits angered her. Steve lived a half-life with excruciating pain, pain like the pain on a cross, and Jane wanted him to be left to let die. Twenty years later Steve is still alive, for I visit him from time to time, still living with pain, still spending many hours of the day sleeping, still being poked and prodded by a medical profession that won't let him die and can't get the medication right.

As a parent I've never had to deal with anything like that. But there are pains other than physical ones. I wonder whether births give us a glimpse into the future? Our first-born, Peter, stormed into the world and his progress through it has been with vigour and not a little noise. David slipped into human consciousness and has lived relatively calmly. Jane was never content. She never gained proper weight as an infant. Dorothy, regularly admonished by the Health Centre sister for Jane's small weight gains, tried everything, even leaving the school boarding house for a week to see if the calmer atmosphere of her mother's home would make a difference. All was to no avail. At four and a half months Jane went onto a bottle, but there was no significant weight gain. Jane wasn't the greedy feeder her brothers had been and I believe a lot of it had to do with her fiercely independent spirit.

Our children were indulged because we hadn't been indulged. And for my part as a parent there was another element involved, the only child syndrome. Unused to squabbling with siblings, only children find open conflict almost impossible to handle. Verbal jousting, strongly expressed differences of opinion and quarrelling appear to these children to be almost deadly. Even now for me in my early seventies, I find criticism and even implied criticism very wounding. After a lifetime, I ought to be able to ride out negative responses but I find it very difficult. I avoid confrontation if

I can and that tendency informed my parenting. I dealt with teenage rebelliousness within the family by being calmly reasonable. I rarely if ever put my foot down, afraid of the risk – as I saw it – of alienating the children. It was selfishness: I didn't want to have to manage objections and refusals and petty angers because they tore at my only-child sensitivities.

Which meant that Dorothy, an eldest child with three younger siblings, had to become the disciplinarian. She stood up to the children in a way I couldn't. It was ridiculous, really. She and I are both Leos, both, according to the stars, determined to lead, made for leadership. I led in lots of things, like which sliced loaf we'd buy or where I'd put the car in a car park (even when Dorothy said, 'There's a space. Park there!'), but I was a weak father. I could be firm, like when Peter failed first year Arts after having gained a Commonwealth Scholarship in Year 12. I told him to leave university instead of staying on to please me. He had really wanted to get into Veterinary Science and his heart was not in his Arts course. But the moral arbiter was Dorothy, forever insisting on truthfulness and kindness and understanding and moral responsibility. She saw the importance of laying them out unequivocally. If there was answering back, she dealt with it better than I could.

Parenting in the 1970s was not easy. Rapid change was everywhere. When Dorothy and I were growing up, we inhabited a known world, known to our parents and known to us. We lived in Christendom. The people we knew were usually church people, or if they weren't were sympathetic to our view of the world. With many we shared certain common views of the world: God, Jesus, right dealing, compassion and so on. Most of us of that generation had known church, Sunday School, Bible Class and church youth group. We used to walk or ride pushbikes. Now, more people had wheels, cars to take them further afield from the local community. Young people began to make friends outside the experience that people like Dorothy and me had had. Our parties were always chaperoned by adults: now parents were taboo at parties.

I especially felt helpless. As a father, I hid behind saying I shouldn't interfere with my children's freedom. Every day at university I was made aware of the new freedom that was in the air. At the same time I didn't want my children to go through times like that period in my own youth when I thought I was operating in God's 'perfect freedom', but I was in fact constrained by all sorts of moral and religious strictures. I wanted my children to be free. I wanted them to become their own persons.

We produced three strong, confident human beings who felt they could take on the world. They were of the generation that fled the nest as soon as they could. Peter, after a year at university, went off to the Riverina as a jackeroo. David took up a residential scholarship in a university college and after a year left for a sequence of student houses shared with friends. Jane went from school into a university college and then she, like her brother, moved into student housing. The university was my world and they felt at home there. So they were free. They all three of them believed in themselves. They were all ready to rescue others. They had a kind of secular commitment, despite their upbringing in church, Sunday school, Bible Class and church youth group. They would have called themselves 'religious': I would have called them religious. They'd be all right, they said. They could take on anything. It was all a bit like my Campaigners for Christ commitment and vision. They took on partners.

The weddings themselves make nice metaphors. David's, the first, was held on the banks of the Hopkins River, near

Warrnambool, and conducted by a young radical Baptist minister (in a red open-necked shirt), who has since left the institutional church. The bride came from a Jewish-Catholic upbringing. Peter's wedding took place in a fashionable Anglican church, with the males of the wedding party in top hats and tails. The bride and bridesmaids were young and beautiful. Jane's, the third and last, was in our living room, because her husband-to-be would have nothing to do with the church, and the ceremony was performed by a celebrant. Three ordained clergymen were present as wedding guests. Jane looked stunning, even regal, as she came downstairs.

It soon became evident that the boys were unhappy. Marriage wasn't turning out to be the strong relationship they thought it would be. No doubt, to be honest, the girls didn't get the marriages they expected, either.

There was a scriptural injunction that the young evangelicals in our room opposite the Adelaide Railway Station used to discuss: 'Be not unequally yoked together with unbelievers'. We discussed it in reference to our girlfriends. And of course there's something in it. Our three children contracted partnerships with people who were unbelievers, not only or merely in a dogmatic religious sense but also in a cultural sense, with people who didn't believe in the same way as they did in literature or music or painting or the reflective life. Or an appreciation of religious transcendence. The togethernesses they'd had initially with their spouses-to-be were exciting and romantic and the whirlwind of their unions made thinking beyond the present quite impossible. Neither side was really prepared to talk their way through to at least a compromise world-view: they simply thought it would work out.

One of the boys lived interstate and the other some distance from Melbourne, so in some ways it was made it easier for us. We didn't regularly have to observe what was happening in their relationships. But with Jane it was different, and here I'm in a dilemma. I find the situation with her wrenchingly painful and it's even worse for Dorothy. When Jane was born, Dorothy's mother, with her Scots dourness, had said, 'Now, dear, I can die happy because you've got a daughter.' But Dorothy hasn't got a daughter. Neither have I. As I was writing this memoir, I was determined to somehow leave Jane out. It was too raw for me to contemplate on the page. I was more than sad, I was forlorn, in despair. I thought I'd cover developments by writing a poem or constructing in a poem an imagined conversation with my daughter. Then I remembered a Fay Zwicky poem called 'Letting Go', in which the poet reflects on the anguish of letting go of children, on the necessity of letting go, with its accompanying grief. Half a dozen lines of the poem almost exactly capture my dilemma:

So you don't write a poem
You line up words in prose
inside a journal trapped
like a scorpion in a locked
drawer to be opened by
your children let go . . .

Here's the journal: Jane married a young lecturer in the university department where she was a Master's student. Initially they lived in Melbourne. Soon tensions arose between us and her husband. I was reminded of the principal character in John Fowles' novel *The Collector*: Jane was being possessed, owned, cut off from her former friends and her brothers. Their first child, a daughter, became bonded with Dorothy in a rare chemistry (daughter's daughter, probably). Each Monday Jane attended a pottery class and we had the little one from mid-morning to early evening. Then Jane's husband took a post at a university in northern New South Wales. During the first year of my retirement we arranged to drive up to see Jane, pregnant with her second child, on her Anzac Day birthday. A letter came informing us that her husband was not yet ready to see us and we shouldn't come. The differences between us issued in arguments, but arguments about what? Not religion, not child-rearing, not anything to put your finger on. The situation was beyond the comprehension not only of Dorothy and me, but also of my two sons and even their wives. We went, anyway, a three day drive. Jane answered our knock on her door and said bluntly: 'What are you doing here? Didn't you get my letter? We're going on holidays in about an hour.'

We drove home crushed. For a hundred kilometres at a time one or the other of us blinked back tears of incomprehension. Over the next five or six years our Christmas and birthday gifts lovingly chosen for the grandchildren were often returned unopened.

Then, sensing an easing of Jane's unaccountable anger, we tried again. Two light-hearted telephone conversations gave us to believe we'd this time be welcomed. And so we were. We were delighted to meet the children, three of them including two we'd not seen before. Dorothy helped dry her much-loved granddaughter's long blonde hair, I did a jig-saw with my grandson, Dorothy read to the youngest. Jane was chattering away to us.

Within four hours – mercifully after the children had gone to bed – it all fell apart. Jane and her husband screamed and ranted at us and he ordered us out of the house. It was nightmarish. On the advice of a local psychologist we stayed in our nearby motel room for several days to give Jane a chance to move towards some resolution, but there was nothing, really. Both she and her husband refused to see the counsellor either with or without us present. The counsellor – we bless him for his compassion and wisdom – recommended we send postcards ('Don't write much. That way what you say can't be misconstrued'). Every six weeks we did, for a year, until a letter from Jane told us the cards and the letters to the children were being thrown unopened into the rubbish bin, and asked us not to write any more.

I can't expect anybody to understand this sorry ordeal. I used to try endlessly to find an explanation but I've given up. It's just unfathomable, beyond comprehension.

Setting this down has been for me very distressing. But it's the key to the drawer where the scorpion waits.

One son, then the next, separated from his wife, each leaving two children confused, uncertain, unsure. I'm not taking sides here, not apportioning blame, just setting down what happened. Dorothy and I have always had our religious position in common and maybe our children, not recognising its importance to our relating, thought marriage would be simple and easy. I'm not going to accept any blame for the lives my children find themselves living. But it all makes me ineffably sad. Knowing my circumstances would be incomprehensible to the majority of other people, or would be regarded by them as frightening or repellent only adds to my pain.

Peter, after years as a sheep station manager, was 'let go' after a company take-over of the property he ran, and acts as a rural consultant in the district where he lives. David, after being director of two regional art galleries, is senior curator of art in a state gallery. They are both very good at what they do. I'm proud of them. I just wish their personal lives had been less complicated.

In the 1980s a book by an American psychologist called M. Scott Peck struck a chord with liberal believers around the world. The book was called *The Road Less Travelled*. Its subtitle, *A New Psychology of Love, Traditional Values and Spiritual Growth*, is a neat summary of what the book is about. It sold in the millions. It touched readers at points of confusion in their lives: it was a no-nonsense honest examination of those things in living that make for fear, grief, hope and love. Scott Peck was unapologetic as he explored what he called dimensions of human experience. On first encounter I thought it a good, helpful book. I could understand its appeal. I wasn't to know that over a decade later Scott Peck would be talking to me.

He published *In Search of Stones* in 1996, though I found my copy years later in a second-hand bookshop in a small country town. It's the story of a three-week trip through the British countryside taken by Peck and his wife in search of prehistoric megalithic stones that became an obsession for them. The author breaks off from time to time to reflect in an intimate way upon his *life*-journey. At one point he's thinking about his three adult children, for he's passing through a painful time.

> It is unclear at the moment whether this is just a very difficult phase or something more permanent. It is also unclear to what extent the problem is due to us being terrible parents, or maybe due to the possibility that we've been almost too good in some ways. And while we are striving for healing, it is furthermore still unclear how much healing is probable or even possible.

Those could be my words, though perhaps written with more despair than I have left in me.

I suffer an on-going sadness because we had three creative

children. Peter paints well when he has the time, which isn't often – we've got two of his strong landscapes hanging on our walls – and he writes well about the milieu in which he's chosen to live. Take this poem, for instance:

When a horse dies under you
the cattle will vanish into the ironbarks
and all that is left are hoofprints in the sand
and steaming trails of dung.

It will heave,
and bloat in rigor until the stench
crashes through the white bubbling nostrils
and drips heavily onto the ground

while you cradle the vacant head.
Sticky with sweat the tufts of hair
on its neck harden in the sun.
Crows gather around the swelling.

A horse is too big to bury
and can't be put away for another time.

And there are David's poems. He's been putting together a sequence based on artifacts and paintings in art galleries. There's this one from one of his overseas research trips:

netherlandish, early 16th century, rosary bead with
the road to calvary and the crucifixion, boxwood,
the metropolitan museum of art, new york.

behind glass
within the vastness of history
the intimacy of reflection

in the mind
within these walnut hemispheres
the whole of the passion
inside
within three centimetres diameter
a city, a populace, horses, children, god
before my eyes
within the reach of memory
wine, gall, tears, death.

And Jane's creativity blossoms in her classrooms – wherever she is (we don't know any more) – and in the things she makes with her hands. We have her pottery about the house. There's one bowl in particular that I love, sandy and sea-blue in colour, with smiling fish swimming around the rim.

I feel sorry for myself when I see all my dreams for my children like wisps of mist in a forest of naked trees. As a child of the Depression I had dinned into me that waste was unacceptable: nothing should ever be wasted. I don't like to think of creativity ever being wasted. Perhaps that's the teacher in me.

I remember once reading a newspaper review that said a play was about 'people hitting the wall as the working class do'. Politically correct though the sentiment may be, it's not only the working class that hit the wall.

How many times have I recited the Lord's Prayer, hundreds? thousands of times? 'Deliver us – that is, me – from evil'. But I can scarcely expect deliverance. The world isn't a place of unalloyed and shining gold. There's disappointment and grief and any variety of agony. I've got friends and acquaintances in the church who hide behind a rather flimsy screen of Christian cheerfulness and pretend that all goes well for them, that they get on well with their children and daughters-in-law and sons-in-law and parents. Often, if they'd only be honest, they hit the wall like most of us do.

My childhood polio experience set up in me an ability to reflect upon what was happening to me, especially the issue of personally perceived injustice. I don't for a moment suggest that my polio was a tragedy. Tragedy is a word we use far too loosely. We talk about a batsman's duck as tragic, a footballer's hamstring injury on the eve of a grand final a 'tragedy'. Aeschylus' Orestes and Shakespeare's King Lear suffer tragedy, and I've never known that intensity of suffering. My polio, however, thwarted me, then, in my splint, and for the rest of my life. To explain its occurrence is a theological exercise, I suppose. The notion that God gave me polio because that's what I deserved is a superficially attractive solution to the problem of evil. God doesn't will misfortune on people, and to suggest our wrong-doing causes our misfortune is a simplistic and limiting explanation. It ends by creating guilt in ourselves, teaches us to blame ourselves and drives us away from God. But the hand of God is not behind everything that happens. It's what we do with what happens to us that matters.

The world isn't fair. I didn't need polio to tell me that, but it was an early indicator to me that that's how things were going to be. That in itself was a good thing. I've never said my experience as a father was unfair. However, I found that my childhood polio experience had a negative influence on the way I came to see the world and the people in it. That is, I was inclined to be too accepting of what happened to me, which sometimes spilled over into a kind of fatalism. If I tried to repair some fractured relationship and found I could make no difference, I would back off, instead of saying 'seventy times seven'. I regret that, but it is now so ingrained in my make-up that I doubt I can do anything about it. On the other hand, my polio experience gave my temperament a positive quality that would enable me to deal with questions of belief. It was a capacity for reflection: later in childhood I would often be accused of dreaming when I was only thinking about something that at the time was important to me. I would become contemplative, would ponder on things, though, it must be said, not always to a conclusion. I've reached no conclusion about the way things have turned out in our lives as a family.

I don't believe I thought I'd escape the Lord's Prayer's 'evil'. If I'd somehow evaded all unpleasantness in life, then my happiness would have been placed in some state of unstable equilibrium by the constant dread of some terrible disappointment just around the corner.

I think that as you actually face pain and despair, not only do you value your happiness more but you are more prepared for unpredictable hurt. It's a bit like being immunised against some disease. We can immunise ourselves against adversity by squarely meeting the unavoidable sharp agonies of life as they come to us. Or that's how it seems to me. Fortune *is* outrageous, as Hamlet reflected. Hiding from it is no solution.

I think I've dealt with the family problems just described not in my own strength. I'm not going to be forced back into the pietistic saying that Jesus my friend stood by me; that's sentimental, and people who would use such an explanation are still in the kindergarten of religion. I will say that the strength I've drawn upon is the strength of love, what as a believer I call the love of God. When I love wastefully, I experience God as the source of love. I go on loving my children and the grandchildren, wastefully, it seems. I have to cope with what, when I'm feeling low, I must admit is bewilderment. I'm bewildered that matters have turned out the way they have. It's as though I can't quite persuade myself that there's nothing I could have done to have made life better. All I've got left is this love that seems to go on welling up.

I love to see the boys when they come home. Their tall frames fill the doorway to the kitchen as they say, 'I've got some phone calls to make, Mum. What time's dinner?' I'd love to answer the doorbell to Jane.

Somebody recently offered us a stylish settee that they no longer had use for and Dorothy and I chorused, 'No, thanks, we're at the stage of getting rid of things, not accumulating them.' Ageing entails letting go of things, involves a stripping away. But I never reckoned on letting Jane go, letting go of the dreams I had for an extended family. It's worse for Dorothy. She was the prime nurturer and in many ways the principal carer. That's just the way it was for most of her generation. No longer, it seems, but that's how it was then. 'Let go,' we said. ' We'll have to let go.' So we have to let go our love or at least recognise that it will not be received. Which scarcely meshes with my theology, it would seem. This, I imagine, is the most painful aspect of ageing.

I've tried to pray my way out of the deep disappointment I feel when I think of the lives of my children. In that sermon on prayer I referred to in the last chapter, the priest said that prayer makes three demands on the one praying: persistence, patience and humility. If the very act of praying is supposed to change me in my attitudes and responses, then perhaps I haven't been persistent enough. I've put the problem to one side because it was too hard. And perhaps I haven't been patient enough, wanting some immediate, magical resolution. Nor, perhaps have I shown humility, which means honesty, surely. I haven't been humbly honest in what I want. What do I want? Some happy, all-forgiving sit. com. of a family? For that would be a denial of the freedom we thought so important for our children.

I'm a rich man, really. We don't have a holiday house or a second car or Internet access (we could have them, I suppose) but life is about choices and we always chose the beautiful and the absolutely necessary rather than competitive acquisitions. But I've had a fortunate life. I never had a hobby for there never seemed to be time for one. Music, reading, but not a hobby. Friends, Dorothy's brothers, all went sailing or fishing, had model train layouts, made furniture, grew roses: I did none of these things. Then, towards the end of my time at the university, Dorothy and I decided to buy a Persian rug in order to link colours in our living room. The rug took hold of me. I read about Persian rugs and was astonished at the complexity of them. I bought a second one. Then I argued that it would be nice to leave one each to our children, so I bought (carefully, even by now knowledgeably) a third. These three rugs form the nucleus of what has become a very modest collection. I became a collector. I had a hobby.

I read about Persian history. I tried to understand the Shi'ite and Sunni split in Islam. I borrowed library books on Persian art and architecture. And I went on marvelling at my little collection of rugs, how they glowed like jewels, how the pile from one angle was dark and shadowy and from another throbbing with colour. Nahavand, Ardebil, Yalameh – the names of weaving centres delighted me. I even spent three weeks travelling through western and central Iran.

From Shi'ite piety comes the idea that a perfection of religion is never totally realisable on earth. One's life alternates between joy and sorrow. Within every moment of joy lies a sorrow in the awareness that this moment will pass. The beauty of every moment of living is touched with an awareness of its impermanence. I'm preparing a new bed in the garden: I dig it over, I fork in sheep manure, I've raked away weeds and I put in my seedlings, marvelling at the gleam of the sun on the damp soil and it's a quiet moment of joy. Then I stop for coffee and where my children are at seeps into my consciousness as I cup the warm mug in my hands.

In my study is a prayer rug from Quchan, a town about 150 kilometres from the holy city of Meshad. In contrast to rugs from western Iran, which are often bright in blues, pinks and reds, ones from the east tend to be in sober browns, olives, maroons. My Quchan prayer rug has a *mihrab* design, that formalised symbolic shape of the gateway to Paradise. I have it pointing, so far as I can guess, in the direction of Mecca out of respect for the sweet-natured Iranians I met in villages and small towns. The prayer rug is finely woven and the pile closely shaved, with a kilim fringe top and bottom. The ground is of the deepest blue and on it are little stylised trees in brown and tan. The human touch is halfway down the right-hand outer border, where the weaver has made a mistake and woven one of his decorative figures the wrong way round.

What's important to me about this sombre, pensive rug is its signifying of where I find myself. The way to Paradise, it seems to be saying, is shadowed, and I know that to be true. However, in the early morning, sunlight lances through the study's windows and when it falls on the rug, the colours leap to the eye. The deep blue sparkles like a spring sky and two hundred tiny trees wave and sway. The rug cries out in joy.

I had to set all this down because I had to be true. This chapter was painful to write and at no point, I swear, did I want to hurt my children or their families, because I love them.

13. Being Human

In an earlier chapter I began to examine what Dad used to say about infallibility in religious experience. Now that I've laid out my disappointments and sorrows as a father, I should return to the issue of what's certain and reliable, incontestable. Certainly not The Church, and not The Book. Dad put it to me that there was a third proposition, that a believer sets principal store by what he or she recognises as the infallibility of human experience. That's where I stand. I find that experience cannot be denied, whether it's physical, mental or spiritual: it can't be avoided. In all our activities we expose ourselves to this human experience. Whenever we take a journey or read a book, go to the cinema or an art gallery or a concert or a football match, we enter into experience. Sometimes, if we're curious by nature, we extend our initial experiences deliberately: for example, we may see a film based on a real-life biography and, after seeing the film, we go to our local library and borrow the book, so enriching and enlivening our experience.

When I was researching the centenary history of a boys' school, I discovered that a house the founding headmaster had built to accommodate the boarders in his growing school was still standing. From the street it looked like any Victorian house of the decade. The fashionable Greek key pattern was laid into the external brickwork and this Victorian kitsch was picked up in the waratah designs in leadlight panels around the front door. The verandah of the two-storey dwelling was typical. Having found the house, I could have got in my car and driven off, satisfied that the house was actually still there.

But, I thought to myself, if the headmaster custom-built the house for his pupils, the interior may be interesting. So I knocked on the door, presented, as it were, my credentials to the occupant, and was invited inside. One would have expected to see a staircase rising as a feature from the hallway. But no, the hall was spacious and long and at its end and to the right the stairs were built out of sight. I could then see how the house had once functioned. There was a large back door. My headmaster's boarders would enter through that back door and could mount the stairs to the four very large rooms above without disturbing the headmaster and his young family, who would have occupied the ground floor rooms. There was also at the rear of the house downstairs a very ample room which would have served as a communal dining room. So this visit of mine serves as a metaphor. Human experience may be had at two levels, the casual and the intimate, to look at the house and to explore it, to have the experience and to extend it.

Strange how things come back to you after thirty, forty years. There was a period in my professional career when I read extensively in sociology. My introductory reading included the work of the early European sociologists, like Emile Durkheim and Karl Mannheim. Now Mannheim returns to me: 'the religious focus is a way of interpreting life from the centre of some paradigmatic experience'. His 'paradigmatic experiences' are those that are highly significant. For our purposes here there seem to me to be four kinds of human experience that are salient and important: the encounter with others; the revelations of the natural world; the inheritance of the past and the experience of existence itself.

Encountering others ranges almost beyond imagining, from meeting the simple and humble to meeting the distinguished and celebrated. I've only ever met two (as they say) seriously famous people. The first was the American novelist, poet, short story writer and essayist, John Updike. I'd been an avid reader of Updike for some eight years when I learned he was coming to Writers' Week at the 1974 Adelaide Festival. Things, of course, can be arranged: a colleague at Adelaide University happened to invite me to give a lecture and a seminar for him that week. So I came to be in Adelaide for the Updike lecture. Now my boyhood friend from chapter one, Bob, also by now an academic, was a skilful networker. He knew someone who was throwing a private barbecue reception for Updike and got me invited. So it was that I said (cheekily), 'Hullo, John,' to the guest of honour. His manner was warm and welcoming, though I'm sure he must have been heartily sick of meeting people he knew he'd never have to see again. I leaped straight in. 'John,' I said, 'One thing. How really important to you is church-going and belief?' His face broke into a wonderful smile. 'No one,' he said, 'has ever asked me that. Important, very important. Why do you ask?' I told him I had a similar Protestant background in Sunday School and church and in his fiction and essay-reviews I felt an answering to my own religious experience. We talked and talked. The following week we met again in Melbourne and had a meal together, and talked and talked. We wrote to each other. I tell of this meeting for two reasons. The first is that the commonality of our belief systems drew us, strangers, into a relationship filled with understanding. The second is that this world-feted author, this universal celebrity, took me as I was, made me feel wanted and important through a quality in himself that I can only call grace.

The other famous person I've met was George Steiner, essayist, literary critic and social commentator. I had for a time been using passages from his *In Bluebeard's Castle: Some Notes Towards a Re-definition of Culture* with my Education students and for my own interest had been reading his collections of erudite essays on language and literature. In 1982 I wrote to him. I told him that I'd be on my way to the University of Venice and that I'd arrange to travel via Geneva if he'd be prepared to see me. Impertinence, it was, I thought. And risky. I knew of Steiner's reputation. He was thought by some to be prickly and pretentious, a relentless name-dropper, arrogant. What on earth would he make of a request from an utter unknown in far-off Australia? But the letter I had back from him was delightfully charming. Of course he'd love to see us (I'd said Dorothy would be with me): let's keep in touch to finalise dates and arrangements. There followed an exchange of several letters, his always warm and friendly. Steiner suggested we sit in on one of his Shakespeare lectures when we arrived in Geneva and we were invited to a seminar the following week on the preface to Wordsworth's and Coleridge's *Lyrical Ballads*. We were to meet him after the lecture. In due course we found our way to the lecture theatre on the given day, and saw this slight figure in a grey suit, one shrunken arm and a very Jewish sharpness of voice. When the crowded lecture theatre emptied, he greeted us elegantly. Could it possibly have been wonderful for him that we were there? And we must have lunch, he exclaimed. We rate that lunch as one of the most pleasant and agreeable we've ever had. Steiner treated us both as equals. There was no trace of superiority on his part, only a genuine concern that we should feel comfortable. We talked, literature, politics, the origin of myth, language, families and children. After lunch we walked him back to his office in the university: he worked from a crammed space about the size of a large broom cupboard. This was a man recognised by the literary world as being one of the century's best-known sages, a polyglot polymath with an unimaginable range. Yet he treated his two Antipodean visitors with a remarkable generosity and human concern. Grace, again.

The goodness of people is a mystery. I've known that goodness in ordinary people, on a bus, in the butcher's shop, over the front fence with a passer-by. Plain, simple goodness. I know the generosity of spirit of a young woman in her late twenties, of a young man in his forties, of an elderly and house-bound woman in her eighties. That kind of goodness will not be confined to age or sex: it simply is.

Evil is a force in human living. I don't believe in evil as Satan 'who is the father of all evil', and in 'his actual existence'. But I have seen evil gleaming in the eyes of another human being and heard it in the voice of another. I've known people who take pleasure in another's pain, who are able by force of personality to set other people against one another, whose meanness of spirit is so pervasive that it shrivels all who come in contact with them. This is evidence of evil that doesn't need wholesale ethnic tensions to demonstrate the satanic. I've sat under the menacing barrage of vituperation from another human being and been convinced, through my hyper-ventilating, that this was evil in action. When I use the phrase the infallibility of human experience, I mean that no one can deny the presence of evil in that experience nor the countervailing presence of goodness.

It concerns me that many churchgoers of my acquaintance find it difficult to admit to evil, or even to face sorrow or grief. They are victims of a sentimentality that believes that if one is saved and has Jesus as Lord, then one is immune to the virus of evil. They come to deny personal pain and anguish in the mistaken idea that to confess to suffering is to let go the protective love of God. They want everything to be *nice*, for the Lord is with them. For them evil is drinking and gambling. In their personal lives all is well because the Lord has blessed them. I've even heard church people say they've never known any stress or pain, never had to confront evil. They are either extremely fortunate or are self-deceivers. To have known the frightful power of evil is not to be without faith. The whole point of Christian belief is that it enables you to see evil and not be overcome by it.

But to return to the mystery of goodness. I count myself fortunate to have been gifted friendship and to have been offered acquaintance with all sorts of people who bore or bear about with them a good character, by which I mean a capacity to enliven and encourage me. These are not the John Updikes and the George Steiners. Thomas Gray got them right in his *Elegy in a Country Churchyard*: 'Full many a flower is born to blush unseen'. I think of the wife of a former colleague who had lost her child in infancy and was godmother to dozens, who was innocent and unsophisticated but utterly loving and whose funeral service was held in a metropolitan cathedral packed with those with whom she'd shared her life and love. I think of a high school teacher, Australian-born but of German parentage, whisked one afternoon from his young family and interned for no other reason than that he had undertaken doctoral studies in Germany, and never did that teacher express anger at his treatment nor harbour any grudge against the authorities. I think of a friend of Dorothy's, who would have once been called 'a fine churchwoman', generous to a fault and with a capacity for entering into the joys of others unlike anyone else we have known, who gave up her well-earned long-service leave to act as secretary to an African bishop so that his secretary could take holidays. There was a suburban general practitioner who never charged any fee for the elderly or needy and for a month every year did emergency medical work in some under-developed country. And if there ever was a 'mute inglorious Milton', it was a colleague of mine whose self-effacing generosity enhanced the academic lives of generations of students and no one knew. We have a friend who lives with crippling arthritis but she produces the most beautiful gold thread embroidery, when every stitch is searing agony for her twisted fingers. A retired academic and his wife always took us into the warmth of their home and their company whenever we were in Cambridge, and made us forget we were visitors.

When I try to define what it is these people have in common I'm forced back to the view they have of existence. All of them have an on-going experience of the Other which in turn alerts them to others. I've come to know scores and scores of men and women who are gentle and kind, self-giving, loyal, charitable, unsparing of time, hospitable, virtuous: they are the human experience. That is infallible. I'm not suggesting that believers have a premium on goodness. I also know non-believers who demonstrate delicate qualities of spirit, compassion, empathy, softness, understanding. That's the point. In being human, the being is shot through with these qualities of goodness, just as silk shimmers colour when it moves. It's just that I take the colours to be of God.

The second paradigmatic experience spins around the revelations of the natural world. I've squatted down with a small grandson and with him watched intently and enraptured as a group of ants struggled to shift a tiny sliver of flesh up an incline and into their nest. At a certain time of the year I've taken a granddaughter around the perimeter of our house looking for the cast-off shells of cicadas and seen her pluck one so delicately from the wall and lay it reverently in her palm. In one of her Religious Education periods

Dorothy wanted to introduce to her girls the idea of awe and wonder. She began by giving each of them a leaf or flower from our garden: they were to look at it closely and then describe it. An activity for pseudo-sophisticated young adolescents? At the end of the period almost all the class members came and asked, some a little sheepishly, if they could keep their leaf or flower. They'll grow out of that, say the cynics. Not my experience of young people, or old. Our sheep station manager son had been known to ring to say that he had watched hundreds of spiders spanning a whole paddock and their webs were shining in the morning light, or to tell us about a beautiful patterning of clouds against the setting sun on the Riverina's broad horizon. Once on a train I fell into conversation with two fellow passengers, man and wife. It turned out they were sheep farmers, like my son. 'Were you up early this morning?' I asked. 'Yair, pretty early. I had some stock to move before we caught the train,' the man said and then he turned to his wife. 'I didn't tell you. You know the paddock behind the Eastern Creek? In all the years, I've never been there in just that spot as the sun was coming up behind the Ranges. In the dawn the mists were rolling over the cliffs and gullies and catching the sun and it was so beautiful.' And he turned to me and smiled.

I can't begin to list my own awe and wonder at the world of nature. Driving at night along a creek bed in the outback Flinders Ranges and seeing the twisted white limbs of the gum trees flashing in the blackness. Sitting on a great boulder etched with orange lichen and listening to wave after wave booming onto an empty beach. Walking along a silent musky track in a forest and watching a jewel-bright blue wren flickering after insects. From the tiny fragility of the wren my mind can scarcely make the connection with super nova and black holes and the two hundred billion stars in our galaxy.

Preparing an address for a school church service once, I rang a physics professor friend. I explained that my theme was awe and wonder, 'Would you, Brian, give me just two amazing facts from the physical world?' He did, without hesitation, and I've been grateful to him ever since. What he told me I incorporated into the address:

> If you were able to take a glass of water and convert each of the molecules in it to a grain of sand, you'd have enough sand to cover the whole of the British Isles to a depth of two feet. That's amazing. But listen to this: if you could enlarge a hydrogen atom to the size of the interior of this church, its one proton and its one electron would each be the size of a pin's head, and all the rest is nothing. That's mind-boggling. And to wonder at that is a step into spirituality.

The inheritance of the past is another highly significant part of one's human experience. This memoir itself represents my inheritance, first of all as a PK. I never became famous as a household name, but I suppose I could claim to have 'got on': I did 'all right'. Clergymen's children, according to one study, appear to be ten times more likely to 'get ahead' than the rest of the population. In Australia notable figures who were parsons' sons include media magnate Keith Murdoch, former Governor-General Sir Paul Hasluck, renowned academic Keith Hancock, former politician John Button, poet A.D. Hope and historians Manning Clark and Geoffrey Blainey. I'm certainly not in their company but I know their inheritance, books, conversation, ritual, other people, commitment. I'll never be able to deny my debt to the family circle in which I grew up. I'm also aware of an ancestry that stretches back and back to where? Strange, but I've always found myself brought up against figures from the past like Albert Schweitzer and William Carey and William Wilberforce and William Cowper (why are they all called William?), all the way back to Bishop Hugh Latimer who at the stake, with the flames already licking at the hem of his robe, cried out to his young companion,

> Be of good comfort, Master Ridley, and play the man. We shall this day light such a candle by God's grace . . . as (I trust) shall never be put out.

Nor has it ever been put out in me. This is what my father meant and what I mean by the infallibility of human experience. There's 'a great cloud of witnesses' to the inescapable Other, to intimations that are (Otto's word) numinous. Men and women down the centuries have been impelled to certain gracious behaviours by this awareness of Something beyond themselves. They have found they are involved in doing and reflecting upon those acts and ideals that have behind them an 'ultimate concern'. I've never thought that this multitude of believers could be wrong. Nor have I thought that only believers are capable of altruism: obviously non-believers as well as believers have contributed to the betterment of human life and affairs. But my reading of the past tells me that many major steps forward in the advance of meaningful community have been initiated by believers, by men and women of God. That sustains me.

The fourth paradigmatic experience has to do with existence itself. It's one thing to reflect upon the goodness and the evil to be found in the men and women we encounter. It's another to consider the simplicities of nature and the infinitude of space. It's yet another to call to mind the past and its cavalcade. But what of existence as an object of contemplation? Our universal and omni-present experience is experience itself. Whenever anything happens to us, that's experience: whenever we go looking for things to happen, we're really after that underived and primary encounter encapsulated in the words: *I am, things are*. The sense of wonder which holds a scientist to his or her researches issues in questions: the physicist or the astronomer asks 'how?' and 'why?' Even the historian is prompted by the questions 'how?' and 'why?' when seeking an explanation for the behaviour of societies in the past. For the believer, however, for the religious person, wonder is sourced in the recognition that men and women exist at all. This realisation of being sets believers wondering at a mystery: that things *are*. There's no point in 'hows' or 'whys'. Ludwig Wittgenstein, one of the knottiest and most influential of twentieth-century philosophers, put it plainly: 'Not how the world is, is the mystical, but that it is'.

At the same time that Wittgenstein was wrestling with the concept of the world, a young German scientist, Werner Heisenberg, was worrying away at atomic functions. Heisenberg proposed his 'uncertainty principle': he claimed that it was impossible accurately to measure both the position and the velocity of a particle at the same time – if you could be certain about one measurement, you couldn't be certain about the other. It seems to my untutored scientific innocence that the uncertainty principle applies from the atomic level up to the functions of the human mind. You can't get everything right at the same time.

Fundamentalists believe you can get everything right all the time. But there can be no such thing as a certainty principle in belief or in living, even. Just as you get one thing sorted out, another goes wrong.

Paul Tillich in his *The Courage to Be*, points out 'the astonishing pre-rational fact that there is something and not nothing'. The most paradigmatic, the most significant thing that I can say about the tall gum tree I can see from the study window is not that it has grandeur or that its timber would be useful for making fence-posts, but that it is. The most profound thing I can say about myself is simply *I am.*

Looking out of the study window during a recent winter I could see through the tracery of bare branches of one of our neighbour's trees great swollen white clouds in the west. They were edged with bright silver from the lowering sun. Two wisps of apricot-tinged cloudlets busied themselves in the palest of blue skies. As I gazed into the immensity behind, I recalled that on our first time in Cambridge we rented Professor Chandra Wickramasinghe's house. Chandra was also a poet. I caught something of his speculations on the nature of the universe from reviews of his work in the newspapers. Now I found the unimaginable behind the clouds dizzying and I dragged myself back into the tracery of tree branches. They were like elegant curling fingers, their bareness beckoning in the spring, yet two months off. Then I was suddenly back at my desk. From the corner of my eye I could see on the filing cabinet a copy of *Roget's Thesaurus*, a volume of *Current English Usage*, and *The Concise Oxford Dictionary of Quotations*. I looked at the back of my broad squarish hand, so like what I remembered of my father's, and marvelled that I am me.

By those words I affirm my existence but I do more than that. I assert that my existence has meaning, that I can distinguish between good and evil, that I share in the spirit of mankind. And once I affirm my own existence, then I cast a vote for positivity in life. Of course there are periods in my life when to make any kind of affirmation is slightly absurd, because of the meaninglessness I encounter. But even in the face of life's negatives, my inner personal centre asserts its right to be.

There are people and matters that in the late afternoon of my life confirm me in my asserting of a believing self. I found it encouraging that in 1986 Les Murray edited a substantial collection (over 300 pages) entitled *An Anthology of Australian Religious Poetry*: the book was reprinted five years later. Then in 1994 came Kevin Hart's selection, *The Oxford Book of Australian Religious Verse*, again substantial (over 260 pages). Two books of religious poetry produced in less than a decade in a so-called secular society? No less than five of the country's widely read poets are unashamedly religious in outlook and expression, James McAuley, Bruce Dawe, Peter Steele, Kevin Hart and Andrew Lansdown; the first four are Catholic, the fifth, Baptist. Or consider Australian novels like Patrick White's *Voss*, that dark journey into resurrection, or David Ireland's *Bloodfather*, about a boy with a Brethren upbringing making sense out of existence, or Tim Winton's *That Eye the Sky*, about the joy of holding on to religious essentials. Literature's been my business, I know, but these poets and novelists are more to me than gifted writers: I have a firmer affinity with them, because their deeps call to mine. In them I find the immanent, the holy, the numinous, the transcendent.

In the last ten or fifteen years I've been trying to relate the richnesses of my experiences with the richnesses of my beliefs. I've met with study groups to explore how the gospel, the Good News, may be seen in poems like Les Murray's 'The Broad Bean Sermon' and 'The Barranong Angel Case', Gwen Harwood's 'ad orientem' or Mark O'Connor's 'The Pairing of Terns', or be seen in short stories like David Malouf's 'In Trust' or Peter Goldsworthy's 'Triple Word Score'. I've talked with groups or at dinner parties about movies like *Babette's Feast*, *Truly, Madly, Deeply* and *Jesus of Montreal*, trying to unravel their significances for believers like me. I can't accept a divide between secular and sacred in this matter: they are of the Whole.

But I find the infallibility of human experience rendered in flesh in my wife, Dorothy. We loved each other deeply and were astonished at how love's depth went down and down as the years passed. We shared, we feared, we rejoiced. We still have a sense of youthfulness in each other. I look across at her as we walk to a concert or to a movie and I marvel at how I feel about her and how I think I'm the most fortunate of men to have her in my life.

She began, as I, with a simple, accepting faith. She'd not been thrust into scepticism as I had and in the early years of our marriage often fell silent at my new-found radicalism. She's a better Christian than I am, in the sense that her believing issues in acts of grace, whereas I'm not of her instinctively generous temperament. She takes in the halt and the lame and it's often only with an effort of will that I join her in her on-going hospitable gestures. She's always checking sick people on the phone to see how they are: I rarely do that. What's infallible is her capacity to love. I've seen it with our own children, sons with chicken-pox, daughter breathless with croup, daughter with a threatened miscarriage, doing without new clothes and perfume for the children's school needs, nursing her dying father in hospital with a tenderness that was saintly, typing and re-typing theses, articles and books for me, researching material by phone and in libraries.

Dorothy is sustained by music. In the middle years of our marriage if I came home to find her playing the piano I knew something stressful had occurred. She always fights the untoward. She always believes things can be better: she never accepts the second-rate. More than anything she wants human relationships to be 'right', within the family, within friendship circles. Really all she wants is what she calls 'civility': she doesn't find a lot of it about. Is she too demanding? Too strong? Expectations too high?

I don't know. All I know is that, after some forty-five years of marriage, she's an exciting and imaginative lover, tender and generous. It's the way she sees our relating that has caused me always to see our physical intimacy as sacramental in the religious sense, never simply two bodies in conjunction. She'll not want all this said: in profound things she's very private. But she has to be included in my human experience, as an infinitely important part of it. As an infallible part of it. For she more than anybody helps me make sense of my often jangling world.

There's my position, then. I believe in the infallibility of human experience. I believe in goodness and evil, for they're revealed to me in the eyes and actions of those who people the theatre of my life. I believe that an awareness of God is to be found in the wonder of creation. I believe that the history of men and women and societies reveals, slowly, a developing consciousness of love and care in human nature. I believe that trying to come to terms with the actual fact of being is an exercise that is self-revelatory.

I realise I'm at odds with Karl Barth, that influential theologian, but I disagree with him. Barth, or at least as I understand him, argues that to search for God in human experience is to confuse him with human life. Barth once famously and aphoristically said, 'You cannot speak about God by speaking about man in a loud voice'. That's not what I'm doing. I'm speaking about the essence of what it is to be human. What I find in humanity is a capacity for goodness and kindness (despite a matching capacity for evil and cruel dealings), and an awareness of a spiritual dimension to living that elevates and ennobles. I find this in human responses to the natural and the metaphysical world and in human dealings with others both in the past and the present. This act of faith of mine, for I suppose I'll have to call it that, isn't readily understandable, especially by people who only value ideas insofar as they are quantifiable and consistent. I know that poems, even *my* poems, are not finally made out of ideas but of words. So it is with faith: faith doesn't come from an ideology but from experience.

Where I find myself in a belief-system is not in receiving some dogmatic set of convictions, the acceptance of which assures the status of faith. It's the other way around. I aspire to a faith-position and then give consideration to a creed. It's human experience that prepares me for belief. Just what those beliefs may be is held over to the next and final chapter in this odyssey.

14. The Story of Two Easters

The first time my first grandson slipped his little hand into mine and we walked down to the park together, I found myself imagining how my family would grow. My other son was married, too, and expecting his first-born. My daughter would surely marry and she'd have children. I began to see myself as a kind of patriarch, surrounded by children, in-laws and grandchildren who would gather in our home on birthdays, at Easter, at Christmas and whenever they could come interstate for a holiday. There'd be laughter and running feet and the big dining table set with colourful napkins. I would preside graciously over the proceedings, hug Dorothy and feel things were good.

In 1989, the second Christmas after my daughter's first baby was born, we were all together, sons, daughter, their spouses, four grandchildren, Dorothy and me. It was a cheerful Christmas Day, unwrapping presents, oohing and aahing, stuffed turkey, brandy-flaming pudding. I wanted a photograph: I rummaged out the tripod I hadn't used for years and with a delayed exposure got us all in. There we were, frozen in time, all laughing or broadly smiling, crowded on and around a sofa. That Christmas we'd bought a fresh tree, elegantly proportioned. It was only about forty centimetres high and we sat it on the library table and covered it with decorations gathered together over the years, some passed down from Dorothy's family, some sent to us from Germany and England at past Christmases. On Twelfth Night we took it down and planted it in the garden so it would be fresh for next year. That Christmas was the last time that we were all together. My dream died and with it Dorothy's. The tree is still in the garden, undisturbed. It's now about 1.7 metres tall. It's waiting for the next Christmas we're all together again. It's our hope-tree.

Thirty, forty years ago I came across an interesting observation of Reinhold Niebuhr's and it's always remained with me. He said, 'Faith only arises when optimism breaks down.' I'm no longer optimistic that our immediate family will be able to share Christmas with us as we grow older, for they have their own problems and difficulties, and with that optimism gone, I only have a faith that one day all will be well. Without that faith I'd go mad.

I always loved reading to my grandchildren when they were small. I did voices, as I had with my own children: for some unaccountable reason I used to give Eeyore in the Pooh stories a lugubrious Welsh accent. I even wrote a children's book for them called *Leonardo, Pigeon of Siena* which was wonderfully illustrated by that charming bear of a man, John Winch. When the grandchildren became independent readers I passed to them books from my children's literature collection (from which I used to lecture). As they entered their teens I joked with them about taking ages under the shower. They keep me young, and what's more, hopeful.

I recently went with Peter's two sons for a walk around the Boroondara Cemetery at the bottom of our street in Melbourne's suburb of Kew. We passed plots for the Sisters of the Sacred Heart and for Jesuit priests, gazed at extravagant Victorian and Edwardian memorials topped with marble angels, lingered in the rows of Italian headstones.

'Gran'pa, what's this funny-looking cross?'

'Russian Orthodox, son,' I replied. 'The extra bit down the upright on an angle, do you mean? Russian Christians believed Jesus' legs were of uneven length.'

'Cool,' he said.

I suppose over the last two or three chapters I've been engaging in an act of denial. I've been pretending that I've been managing my spiritual life through reading and quasi-theological contemplation, when in fact I haven't been managing at all well. Thirty years ago I wrote a poem entitled 'At Times':

At times (usually when I feel least poetical)
I look down the narrowing shaft of my self
and can see nothing but the narrowing, the precipitous sides:
somewhere there ought to be, not this gulf,

but a dim myth-face, to answer my eyes.
I hear things, or half-hear, rather:
organ music in a rococo church, the bump
of herring baskets on a quay, altogether

unrelated sounds barely heard.
Yet the shaft is not for listening at.
I want to see some face. Mine
I seek at the bottom of this great sharp pit.

I re-read it and I find I still can't quite see some face. I want to see *my* face. There's a terrible story I once read in a book by some psychiatrist, about a patient who looked in a mirror and could see no reflection of himself. I'm not suggesting my concept of self is as pathological as that, but I sometimes (usually when I feel least poetical) wonder why I feel, well, bereft.

These last ten years have been full of experiences I'd not dreamt of and some were related to the writing commissions Dorothy and I undertook together. These experiences I would have to categorise as epiphanies, deep intimations of the Other, that transcendence that breaks into my person too often to be merely ephemeral.

Our researches for one book took us to north-west Poland to a village called Klepsk. A pot-holed road led between barns and houses to a church with an interior that was a revelation, a phenomenon. Walls and ceiling were covered in paintings, portraits of prophets and the apostles, narrative pictures of bible stories. The organ pipes were set in an extravagant gilt case. Over the sanctuary was a barrel-vault, sky-blue, with stars, and set with medallions representing the promises of God. The late seventeenth century came alive in all its baroque exuberance. The Russian babushka who acted as caretaker told us of the church's restoration during Word War II, to us an almost unbelievable notion. Then she told us the church was a museum: no one worshipped there any more. But the glory of the place still spoke to us.

We went to north-west Australia to the Buccaneer Archipelago for another book. A float plane from Broome flew us over 260 kilometres and countless islets and islands to a cove outside Coppermine Creek. Not far from the pearl farm we were visiting is a narrow passage between islands which, at the turn of the ten metre tide, becomes a series of churning whirlpools. One afternoon we went there in dinghy with an outboard motor. As the tide turned, at first there were circles of tiny whirlpools like the footsteps of insects dimpling the surface of the water. Then larger swirls three and four metres across began to turn the dinghy in circles. With the motor cut, I could hear the deep murmuring of the tide. Wherever I looked there were downward-sucking whirlpools and beneath the green-blue surface of the water was an eight-knot tide rumbling out to sea. It was like a submarine thunderstorm. The might of the tide was beyond imagining. I thought of *mysterium tremendum*. Otto wondered whether *tremenda majestas* wasn't a better phrase. I felt it there, in that swirling water, the amazement of being alive and sensing and feeling. This was me facing sublimity.

There have been other experiences too, that were scarcely epiphanies. I wonder how to match them up. It's rather like Dorothy and me going to an orchestral concert. The program gives us Haydn and Corelli, or Elgar and Sculthorpe, and we're content. We understand and know how to respond. Then we have an avant-garde symphony. This music is dissonant, jarring, loud with four timpani players, atonal, turbulent and thick. We don't understand and don't know how to respond. We have no right to expect a program to be tailor-made to our preferences, but unfortunately the discordant, jangling music gets in the way of our response to the rest of the program. This concert is a metaphor of the last ten years.

I don't want to lay any more on the memory of my father, but he's at least part of my life-sense of loss. I suppose that when nearly ten years ago I retired, I thought living would take a new turn. I'd be free, Dorothy and I would be free to see children and grandchildren, free to indulge them with our love, and it's turned out that both distance and an unwillingness in one instance to want to share grandchildren has meant that our love cannot be given in the way we'd hoped. Had we given too much love and was there a surfeit of it? I can't go on searching for explanations. The great fact is our great aloneness. What caring capacity we possess is now dissipated among the frail and elderly and a surrogate family. It's not what I'd dreamed about, but I guess it's all I'm, we're, going to get. 'Thou art with me, Thy rod and Thy staff they comfort me': can I say with Dad, 'Put it away. I know all about that'?

My sons tell me often, now, that they were privileged in their growing years in a way they only now have come to understand. They felt secure, they say, and able to take on the world. But my daughter is lost to us, as are her three children, largely, I suspect, because her family ties were too much for her husband to bear. We have been told, Dorothy and I, that we are a formidable couple. We don't see this ourselves, but maybe the strong bonds of our love were a threat to members of our extended family. I'll never really know the answer to that.

Our children grew up at just the worst time. On the world stage were lies and shocks, the massacre of Israeli athletes at the Munich Olympic Games, Richard Nixon cheating his country. At home, dissent was widespread, authority questioned on all sides, and youth became politicised. In schools and universities there were symbolic acts of rebellion, vandalism, drunkenness, drug-taking, minor theft. It was the Me Generation.

So with our children there's no dropping in with a takeaway pizza on a Friday night or having a family roast with us on Sunday. We now have seven grandchildren, three of whom we never see, four we see occasionally, usually two at a time. The pain of this is often too much for us to bear and we cling to each other in desperation. Our friends and acquaintances seem surrounded by their extended families ('the grandchildren are with us this week') and we ask ourselves that ridiculous question 'Why is this happening to us?' One of my former colleagues, a PK like me, knows how it is: his wife once said to me on the phone (I've changed the names), 'Michael's into his second marriage, Angela's a lesbian and Margaret's husband has just walked out on her with her best friend, so we think we're a pretty normal family.' They were good parents and liberal believers, as we think we were. Why? None of our children go with any regularity to church, nor do our grandchildren. I don't suggest we're the only parents in this generation to know loneliness. Many parents in their late sixties and seventies have experienced similar situations but even knowing that doesn't diminish or remove the anguish and puzzlement. Was it what I believed, perhaps, or didn't believe? Or what I believe now?

There are people who don't question life at all. There are those who come from a non-believing background and when they embrace a faith-position they accept everything. There are those who lose whatever religious beliefs they had because life doesn't mesh with their simplistic religious view of the world. And then there are those who wrestle with the difficult issues that confront them, trying to see them and to make sense of them through a faith-belief perspective. Some wrestle and give it all away because it's too hard.

There's no point finally in setting down what I *don't* believe: what I don't believe doesn't really matter. I don't believe in the Biblical creation story except as a rich myth; I don't believe in the Virgin Birth or the heavenly choir in the Bethlehem sky except as a bridge to Old Testament prophecy and imagery; I don't believe heaven is a place we go to according to the quality of our living, there for the blessed to live with Jesus for ever. These things don't matter a jot in my belief system, because believing in them doesn't really have any effect upon my essential relating to God. People in the Church still make of prime importance things about which Jesus said nothing.

I believe in God. I don't conceive of God as some super being external to life. That's a serious problem: someone once said that if horses thought of God, he'd look like a horse. So with us. We want to anthropomorphise this ultimate being as the Greeks did with their gods and God turns out to look something like General Booth of the Salvation Army. And in space, somewhere. That's not my God. My God is a divine process coming into the throbbing life of the world. A.N. Whitehead (my favourite educational philosopher) saw God, he said, as existing in all of reality and expressing himself by absorbing and transforming all that happens in the world of time and place. This God, therefore, is the on-going source of newness and contingency, of hopefulness and possibility. *That* I can believe.

The height image of God dies hard. Preachers still talk of 'the vertical dimension' in Christian living and that's not helpful: it reinforces, however subtly, the up-there, out-there on a throne of judgement image of God. We have to call *up* to him. For me, I find him just at my elbow. Paul Tillich's ground of being makes sense for me. The God-process, to be meaningful, has to enter into the whole of existence, providing the base for belief. When I listen to Schubert's String Quintet, I know there is something beyond bricks and mortar and clocks. There is a realm of Spirit. There is something not bounded by the pulse of blood in my body and the electrical charges in my brain. My body can't grasp it nor can my brain. It *is*. It transcends experience. And I choose to call this Otherness God. It's this process-God that leads the human spirit (my spirit) out of captivity into the promised land.

The whole business of religion is shot through with paradox. When I speak of the transcendence of God I've got in mind that which is both beyond and near. The beyondness is not remoteness but is in a cosmic swing of grace. When I speak of the immanence of God I'm similarly faced with intellectual and spiritual danger. For it's possible (lots of believers do it) to so stress the nearness of God that he/she (what pronoun?) becomes some kind of warm friend. My experience tells me that the immanent God is one whose continual presence is not only comforting but at the same time demanding. We can never escape the immanence of God. That is, if the transcendence of God isn't about remoteness, then, equally, his immanence isn't about feeling cosy. God is wholly other, yet always present, and this paradox is at the heart of Christian belief.

I keep using the word 'belief'. It's probably about time I began using the word 'faith'. People like me who believe in God are commonly described as 'having faith'. However, faith isn't quite the same as belief. Faith is a kind of conviction or commitment which I can't perhaps explain to those who don't share my commitment. The basis of faith may be more difficult to communicate than the basis of belief. What is an intellectual domain (belief) becomes linked to a highly personal domain (faith). It's common practice, and I'm guilty of this, to use the terms interchangeably when dealing with issues of religion, but one (belief) comes before the other (faith). For me to have faith I have to first believe, and I can't blindly believe anything; I must find experiential grounds for belief.

Let me try and explain with an example. We're tempted to make as it were graven images of God; that is, turn our own mental pictures of God whatever they may be into replacements for the reality of God. I believe that. Now, when we meet our fellow men and women, we are reminded that, as G.K. Chesterton observed, God in creating them broke his own law and made a graven image of himself, the one and only image through which he's willing to be encountered. I think I believe that. Therefore what we encounter in other people isn't what we imagine of God but is God in reality. Other people are the images through which we may meet God. I have faith that that is the case.

I haven't explained it very well, have I? God? I believe in God? I have faith that God is? Thomas Aquinas said that we know God best when we come to the point of knowing that we don't know him.

I believe that the process that I call God was enfleshed in a Palestinian called Jesus. The incarnation is the first and primary given of Christianity. The traditional view is simple. God 'came down' to Earth in the form of a little baby who grew to become a teacher and healer and finally was crucified by his enemies, his death 'a propitiation for our sins' and his resurrection a promise of everlasting life for all. Much finer minds than mine have tried to come to terms with the concept of the incarnation. All I can do is put down the view that satisfies my need for comfort in a world that would otherwise appear senseless.

My father (will I never escape his shadow?) said to me once, when I was in my late teens, that Jesus was either God made man or man made God, and he (my father) was agnostic on the matter. He just didn't know, and wondered whether it was important, anyway. There's the problem, of course. Was Jesus human or divine or some strange amalgam of both? It's simplistic to fall back on that rather slick comment that it wasn't that Jesus wasn't able to sin but that he was able not to sin. We can't have it both ways. If Jesus was both human and divine, this would suggest some kind of continuity between things divine and things of humanity. Mentoring me through his books, the Cambridge theologian Don Cupitt ('conservative Christianity is a contradiction in terms', he once wrote) has helped me on this issue. Cupitt argues that the real subtlety and freedom of Christianity's message rested upon the way Jesus perceived with a sharp irony the disjunction between the things of God and the things of men. That is, Jesus constantly juxtaposed two ways of being, contrasting value sets in order to make his hearers aware of the transcendent:

> It underlies (writes Cupitt) Jesus' paradoxes of righteousness and unrighteousness, loss and gain, death and life, poverty and riches, the manifest and the hidden, security and insecurity, prudence and folly, and justice and injustice. The essential thing is that the two contrasting orders must collide.

The conservative doctrine of the incarnation somehow unified what Jesus kept in contrast. I find that idea difficult to accept: you can't unify righteousness and unrighteousness, security and insecurity, justice and injustice. You have to *choose* and that simply cannot mean choosing between God and Jesus: that's unthinkable. So we're now treading very deep water.

My way out of it is this: God is a process of transformation in the created world. That same mind of God, in the greatest mystery of all, lodged in the flesh of this Jesus, to accelerate creation's transformation. That satisfies me. I don't need any more than that. And there is something further. This incarnation in Jesus was the first, most dramatic and most complete. Jesus entered into the mind of God; the mind of God entered into Jesus. But there have been subsequent incarnations in what I choose to call God's ultimate will. From Latimer at the stake there's been an extraordinary 'cloud of witnesses' touched by that same mind, even to the last fifty or sixty comparatively recent years: lives like those of Edith Stein, Dietrich Bonhoeffer, Martin Luther King Jr, and Oscar Romero were lived out under the paradoxes of Jesus and these paradoxes took them to the gates of death, the way Jesus went. For me, the incarnation stands for the way God's mind and will breaks into the world.

With the essences of the life and ministry of Jesus I have no difficulties at all. His life is remarkable in its vigour and lack of compromise: he is open to all he meets, young children, women, the poor and the wealthy, the blind and the mad. Jesus tells me other people are important, are of value. He tells me that created nature and grace are reconciled: God *is*. And he tells me where to find God. G.M. Hopkins puts it the best of anyone I know in his poem 'As Kingfishers Catch Fire':

. . . the just man justices;
Keeps grace: that keeps all his goings graces;
Acts in God's eye what in God's eye he is –
Christ – for Christ plays in ten thousand places,
Lovely in limbs, and lovely in eyes not his
To the Father through the features of men's faces.

The life of Jesus is full of twists and turns: there are the stories he tells, about sparrows that die, and aggrieved trade unionists demanding more pay, and most wonderful of all, about a son that was lost and is found. There are his dealings with people, going to supper with a social outcast, tying jealous rabbis in knots of argument, greeting a woman's entreaties with silence, healing lepers and they go off with only one thanking him.

One major incident in Jesus' life that I find important is what is called his transfiguration. Mountains are important in scripture as places of revelation. Up Mount Hermon go Jesus and three of the disciples: the mountain is over 3000 metres high, snow-covered for eight months of the year. Exhausted from the climb, the disciples collapse in the heather and doze while Jesus goes on to a higher ridge where he prays. When the disciples wake, they see Jesus transfigured, metamorphosed, dazzling white, shining like burnished metal and there were two figures, one Moses (they thought), one Elijah. Then a cloud descends: clouds, like mountains, are important in scripture. And a voice comes from the cloud: 'This is my son: Listen to him'. If we admit to a spirituality at the centre of our lives, then, irrespective of our theological understandings, there'll be times when we have moments of insight, transfiguration experiences. I've known such experiences. One I remember clearly because I wrote a poem about it later. It was sunset on the plains near Wentworth in New South Wales. Right around the horizon for 360 degrees, there was a sweep momentarily of an orange-pink glow, right around me wherever I looked. 'It was good to have been there': it was transfiguring. Like I've known in an orchestral concert or at the cinema or coming in to land in an aeroplane at dusk, or simply reading. But there are deeper transfiguration experiences. The Martin Luther King Jr 'I have a dream' speech began 'I've been to the mountain top'. Concerts and films can't match the gleaming whiteness of transfigurations like that. But transfigurations do come to us. The metaphor of it is plain.

Which leaves me with the resurrection and the Second Coming. The resurrection stories are too confusing. There's a great stone rolled away from a sepulchre, there's an angel, there's Jesus re-appearing from a cloud, walking into a locked and barred room and so on. What the New Testament writers were trying to do in their figures of speech was to show that the 'process-God in Jesus' was an indication of the destiny available to his followers on acceptance of the Holy Spirit. After the death of Jesus, the disciples were alive in a new way because he was now a reality manifested in them, 'for Christ plays in a thousand places,/Lovely . . .' as Hopkins put it. The literal-minded in later generations transformed that spiritual discovery into stories about Jesus' physical resuscitation. Ideas like 'Death is swallowed up in victory' were current as I was growing up; 'we shall not sleep but we shall all be changed, in a moment, in the twinkling of an eye, at the last trumpet'. Physical resurrection is still held to by conservatives: I read recently in a slim volume of missionary reminiscences of a mission convert who had died and was 'up in Heaven with Jesus'. What else can that mean but some replica of the dead person walking the golden streets of heaven with his Lord?

Of course Death can't afford to be proud (John Donne's phrase) because death isn't the end. Or so I infer from the Jesus story. My father lives in me. I live in my son. I live in my daughter. My grandson lives in my son. My father lives in his great-grandsons, his great-granddaughters. I believe people live on in the lives they've touched and in the memories that people have of them and in a greater consciousness. And so on. I've written already about the mind of God and the process-God. I further believe that in the infinite mind of God we all live on totally and forever. The infallible memory of God holds us. This is our immortality, the books of our lives filed away. Charles Hartshorne puts it well:

> Death writes 'The End' upon the last
> page, but nothing further happens
> to the book by way of either
> addition or subtraction.

That is how I cope with resurrection as a concept. However, I have a more positive view of the after-life than Hartshorne would appear to have expressed here. To pursue his metaphor. *I* believe the book of my life will go on being read by the mind of God and render service through his grace to a part of the transformation of the world. I believe I shall go on living my life and contributing eternally to the consciousness of God, as did Jesus.

And the Second Coming? Jesus has already been. He's done his work. He didn't make the mistake. We did. We, the Church, thought, because the early believers thought it, too, that Jesus had come to establish the Messianic Kingdom and conquer the world. He didn't do that: he set up no politico-military empire. So to do that he'd have to come again. But I think that's not it at all. Eschatology, the doctrine of the last four things, death, judgement, heaven and hell, has clouded too many minds. God-as-judge is open to all sorts of literal interpretations, but God-Jesus doesn't have to 'come again' to judge me: I am judged before him daily.

I've said nothing about prayer and praying, at least as a spiritual exercise. There's no point in praying about the weather, I believe, or a friend with cancer or whether you should change your job or not, in the expectation that the prayer itself will make a difference. That's not the area where prayer operates. Prayer doesn't change things, as the evangelical bumper-stickers claimed. However, the fact that I, in prayer, relate to God and his spirit of goodness and grace means that I am thereby changed, that my relationship with the Other is affirmed. Then it may come about that I, thus affirmed in the Other, may make a difference, be able better to cope in myself with a flood or encourage someone seriously ill or make a long-term judgement about a career move. As liberal believers used to put it in the 1930s and 1940s, 'Prayer doesn't change things. Prayer changes me and I change things.'

Nevertheless I have to admit to being tempted to believe that there is a world of spirit amenable to change by the world of the physical. As Shakespeare's Hamlet said, 'There are more things in heaven and earth, Horatio,/Than are dreamt of in your philosophy', and as Tennyson put it in 'The Passing of Arthur', 'More things are wrought by prayer/Than this world dreams of', so I'm at least inclined to think of prayer as, if you like, a psychic phenomenon. There are too many honestly attested cases of praying reaching from one person to another or from one group to another for me to dismiss its probability. So, I just don't know, intellectually, I have to suspend that kind of judgement. Even if I don't *know*, I want to *believe*.

The writing of this book was, I thought, a desire to resolve the conflict of issues in my belief system. If I could set down something of my religious adventure it would affirm me in what had become important to me. I told myself I wanted to reach all those other believers in exile and tell them it was all right, that there were lots of people just like them. But it's turned out to be not only that. It's also been about Dad.

Have I without recognising it been seeking some kind of reconciliation with my father? In that lecture of John Updike's I went to in Adelaide, the novelist suggested that we write not only from memory but also from latency. That is, it's not only from things we've actually remembered that we find material for our books, but also from things that haven't yet happened. So am I meeting Dad for the first time?

He was a silent, reserved, inward creature. I think he chose not to talk about personal things because he thought he wouldn't be understood. He never felt he could afford to be vulnerable with me. This was his generation and his fundamentalist upbringing. *His* father would never have revealed anything of himself to *his* children. Therefore Dad thought it inappropriate for him to be open with me. I'd have been the same, I think, except that I had a wife who insisted I talk intimately both with her and with our children.

On top of all the hideous trench warfare, internalised but never properly processed, Dad had his own tragedies that drove him to silence. He saw himself as a 'minister': in his ministering he took on the pains and fears of his congregations and this added depth and intensity to the shadows in his life. It's so true that the clergy often carry more than one person can reasonably bear and it's people's expectation that they will manage their own lives. It's a very deep regret I have that Dad never felt free with me. 'Good, son'. That was all. I wonder where the life, ministry and message of Jesus was in all this.

Perhaps I do part-mirror my father. I'm often silent and inward. Not always. Sometimes. But if there's one thing that binds us (apart from a close physical resemblance which has passed from me to one of my sons and one of my grandsons) it's the notion, belief in, acceptance of the infallibility of human experience. Except that it meant something different to each of us. For Dad, it was a kind of code to break into his personal amalgam of inwardness and stoicism, whereas for me, it's a code of acceptance. Yet in a strange and even mysterious way, the two concepts meet. My father and I meet. We are reconciled. God the Father? Abba?

John Updike was surprised when I met him that Adelaide evening with a question about his church-going. He should not have been, though maybe unbelievers were embarrassed to raise such matters. He should not have been: apart from the Protestant church-going that lies at the back of so many of the novels and short stories ('The Deacon' is a most moving story), Updike has also written on the work of theologians like Paul Tillich, Denis de Rougemont and Karl Barth (in fact, the novel, *Roger's Version*, deals with a young computer hacker who believes God's existence can be proved and who has extended discussions with a divinity professor who is a follower of Karl Barth). Updike makes no secret of his religious sympathies. A regular contributor to the *New Yorker*, Updike was recently commissioned by the journal to write an extended essay on the future of faith. It's a beautiful piece, and in it he remembers tenderly how, as a teenager, he took up the offering in church with his Sunday School teaching father. The memory prompts him to observe:

> It is difficult to imagine anyone shouldering the implausible complications of Christian doctrine without some inheritance of positive prior involvement.

I do understand that. I wonder whether I'd have been able to manage belief and faith had I not had 'positive prior involvement' in the life of the Church. This doesn't mean, however, that I am unaware of the 'mysterious way' God performs 'his wonders' in the lives of those who have no inheritance of belief. That is just as remarkable as the fact that I'm still a believer, albeit in exile.

Perhaps Updike deals best with this problem of belief in his story 'Pigeon Feathers'. In it teenaged farm-boy David is struggling with 'implausible complications'. He asks his Lutheran pastor in a catechism class about Heaven and is told it is 'like Abraham Lincoln's goodness living after him'. Which David doesn't find at all helpful. The boy worries away at belief, wanting to find some certainty. At the end of the story, he's asked to shoot the pigeons that are infesting the barn and when he collects the birds' bodies and lays them together, he marvels at the infinite variety of colour in them, the intricacy of the feathers, the rapturous wonder of them. And it comes to David that if God could lavish such care on these vermin, then he would never cease to care for him. For the boy, a certainty to hold on to, to believe in.

But I can't not include here another reference to George Steiner. In 1995 he published an essay entitled, 'Two Suppers'. It's a comparison and contrast between the Socrates supper in Agathon's house and the Last Supper of our Lord, the violence done to Socrates in 399 BC and to Jesus in 33 AD. What I find remarkable about this study is the way Steiner's human sensitivity and his elegance as a literary critic all but transcend his Jewishness as he examines John 13:21–30. It's the most subtle, thought-provoking and engaging analysis of the passover meal that I can imagine. At one point Steiner writes:

> With incomparable dramatic subtlety, the author of John interweaves, as it were, mental and material opacities. Jesus is 'troubled in spirit'. The resonance is vividly human . . . The disciples look at one another perplexed both as to his precise meaning and personal designation. What betrayal? By whom? The drama of the situation, which innumerable painters and composers have striven to express, hinges on the seating order and the respective distances from the speaker.

There's an idea. And Steiner's right, of course. Peter's too far away at the table really to hear what's being said. And what other significances may we find in the seating arrangements? It's just these kinds of intimacy of detail that make the Jesus story endlessly and eternally fascinating. Here, I have to thank a gracious Jew for delighting me in my believing.

Thank him, yes. I am thankful, and for a myriad experiences. The words I have to use are 'I thank God'. I thank that transcendent and transcending process I call God for the living I've known. I have a great sense of gratitude for life itself, for just being alive, for places I've been, for kids I've taught, for caring friends, for extended family, for Dorothy, for having been able to think and feel through to where I've got to. Sometimes it gets too much for me, this sense of gratitude and I get a strange thick sort of feeling in my chest. It's the kind of lyrical delight in e.e. cummings' lines

i thank You God for most this amazing
day: for the leaping greenly spirits of trees
and a blue true dream of sky; and for everything
. . . which is infinite which is yes

(i who have died am alive again today . . .

By the time I took early retirement from the university, Dorothy and I had co-authored two educational histories and had embarked on a third: word of mouth was getting us commissions. The third was the centenary history of a Lutheran secondary school in Adelaide. Becoming involved in the history brought back all those names like Pfitzner and Schulz and Auricht from my growing up. As we were nearing its completion, we had the silly and romantic idea of travelling to the former Prussia, where the original German settlers had come from. Before we set off for the old Brandenburg region we stayed with one of the school's old scholars, now a Lutheran pastor in a parish on the outskirts of Bayreuth. It was Easter. In the central aisle of the profusely baroque church was placed on Good Friday a rough cross of fir timber, the naked wood flecked with bark. A crown of thorns hung from it and a black drape. The pastor's wife whispered to us that the wood for the cross came from the church's Christmas tree of four months earlier. That was a powerful symbol. For in the manger story the magi had brought gold, frankincense and, let it not be forgotten, myrrh, the anaesthetic drug the crucified Jesus refused to take. In the service, much store was set by silence: *Stille Gebet* said the printed order, *Stille*. Come Easter Day, the stark Good Friday cross was now behind the altar, covered in entwined fresh greenery and white daisies, the sudden signs of Spring. As the worship began, the choir in the balcony sang a joyful, modern *Alleluia* and the organist thundered a Bach toccata of celebration. This Easter time was rich in religious dignity, calm, steady, thought-provoking, full of hope.

Some months before we left for Germany, Patricia Kailis, who'd been bridesmaid at our wedding, visited us in Melbourne. She'd married a Greek-Australian maritime entrepreneur in Western Australia. When she learned we were going to Europe she suggested we join her and husband Michael in Greece for a holiday after our Lutheran project was completed. So it came about that four weeks after our Western Easter in Bayreuth we found ourselves celebrating the Orthodox Easter on a tiny Dodecanese island where Michael's family had come from.

Castellorizo is tucked under the Turkish coast, the easternmost of the Greek islands. It's a fairy-tale place, but, sadly, home now to only two hundred inhabitants. But at Easter Castellorizians and their descendants come home: the island is suddenly and vibrantly alive. On their Good Friday afternoon, in the Cathedral of Saints Constantine and Helene, mothers and young girls are decorating the church and the carved representation of Jesus' tomb with garlands of flowers. In the evening as we arrive for worship, there is a din in the church: two choir groups chant, people have conversations, children play. We're blessed with perfumed holy water and four servicemen (the island has a permanent garrison) take guard at the Jesus tomb. Hundreds of candles flicker. The congregation joins the choirs in singing and then the sepulchre (the *epitaphion*) is borne shoulder high from the church and down the rocky roadway to circuit the little township. We are tired from a week's fasting. At twelve noon the next day the church bells suddenly and frantically ring out. Shots are fired, thunder-flashes go off and the explosions reverberate around the grey and white bony hills. For according to Orthodox belief, this was when the stone was rolled away from the Lord's tomb. The bangs go on for an hour. That night in the church the sweet smell of incense lifts the choirs' chanting into the grand chandeliers. Suddenly the priest flings open the door of the iconostasis and enters the sanctuary, holding aloft three lit candles. Joyfully the worshippers light their candles from his and follow him into the cathedral courtyard, crying *Christos anesti*, Christ is risen, to each other. Now the Dionysian quality of Orthodox worship explodes: fireworks splutter and boom, there are flares and sky rockets and Catherine wheels and the church tower shudders with the fierce ringing of the bells. *Christos anesti*.

These two Easters together cover as it were the map of my belief system: they represent where I'm at. I've journeyed my scriptural three score years and ten and find that I'm at a place where I can still almost burst for joy, where I find causes for laughter and cheerful responses, sky rockets and Catherine wheels. But in the same place (paradox, yet again) I find calm, constancy and *Stille*, space for reflection.

With David's son and daughter I can sit for an hour or more while the three of us read. There's no chatter, simply the concentrated quiet of reading. But some months back Dorothy and I took them to New Zealand for a holiday. I rode the Shotover Jet with them, a jet boat that roared at heaven knows how many knots through a narrow, boiling ravine and did complete turns at speed so that we were drenched with the spray and yelled and whooped in excitement.

I'm seventy-three. I'm on the fifth. As I straighten up after teeing my ball, something catches my eye. Above me is a pelican, looking like a Catalina flying boat, gliding steadily across the blue of the sky. I settle at the ball, take my accustomed pause, swing and half turn and on a satisfying thwenk! I see the ball fly high and straight, dead straight down the fairway and run and run along the silent grass. And it suddenly comes to me that A.B.L. White would have been so pleased with the shot. A.B.L. White, Sunday School Superintendent. Part of my inheritance of prior positive involvement in the implausible complications of belief.

I've not covered in this confession all the things I believe or don't believe. That would be too crowded a memoir. I've not set down where I stand on the doctrine of salvation and sin and all the rest. All that's here are what I feel are the essentials. I could make a case for women in the church, an issue that I've felt strongly about ever since an avowed lesbian minister baptised one of my grandsons with such gentle and stylish worshipfulness. I could make a case for the acceptance into the church of homosexuals generally, because they are as much children of God as any. But this is not where I want to argue any case on the grounds of justice. This is where I want to state the basic outline of my believing.

I've travelled a road from fundamentalism to what I take to be a defensible position within critical liberalism: two generations of Australians like me have made that journey in a throbbing and tumultuous period of economic depression, war, the rebellion of youth, unsettling ideas and global information technology. My very being on that road has been a process of becoming. I'm reminded of something from a character in Peter Brook's stage version of the Hindu epic, *The Mahabharata*: he's talking about the importance of story, and says, 'If you listen carefully, at the end you'll be someone else.' All I've been doing is listening carefully.

I have to return to the *ichthus*, that fish symbol of two simple curved lines, one concave, one convex. One of those lines for me (this is the naked fish, with no decorations or accretions) represents God Leading, leading me out of whatever country would have choked me and into a Promised Land of limitless vistas. The other line represents God Coming, coming in the personhood of Jesus and in the guise of other people of grace, coming continually circumstance to circumstance.

In the 27th chapter of the Acts of the Apostles, Luke gives an account of shipwreck off the coast of Malta. Paul and a number of other prisoners were being taken by sea to Italy and the squat little tub, with 300 persons on board, had been for days battered by fierce winds and high seas. Eventually, when in sight of land, the crew tried to pass between the land and a small off-shore island, the ship ran aground on a mud-bank and stuck fast. Waves thumped on the deck and tugged and thrust at the hull until the ship sprang leaks and began to break up. Then, as Luke put it in his narrative, 'some on planks and some on other things from the ship . . . all escaped safe to the land'.

In the process of writing this book, I know I've often fallen back on figures of speech, particularly metaphors to help me say what I wanted to say. So here's another metaphor from this sailor's tale. The ship of my faith had been under the stress of storms for a long time and finally began to break up. In the tumult and hubbub, in the turbulence and commotion, the pain and disappointment, the grief and the bewilderment, I'd been flung into the stormy water and had to grab hold of something to keep me afloat. What this book's been about is the planks and other things from the ship that saved me from drowning. Clinging to *them*, I believe I'll make it safe to the land.